Copyright © 2011 XAMonline, Inc.
All rights reserved. No part of the material protected by this copyright notice may be reproduced or utilized in any form or by any means, electronic or mechanical, including photocopying, recording or by any information storage and retrievable system, without written permission from the copyright holder.

To obtain permission(s) to use the material from this work for any purpose including workshops or seminars, please submit a written request to:

XAMonline, Inc.
25 First Street, Suite 106
Cambridge, MA 02141
Toll Free: 1-800-509-4128
Email: info@xamonline.com
Web: www.xamonline.com
Fax: 1-617-583-5552

Library of Congress Cataloging-in-Publication Data

Wynne, Sharon A.
    CSET English 105, 106 Practice Test 1: Teacher Certification /
    Sharon A. Wynne. -1st ed.
    ISBN: 978-1-60787-161-3
    1. CSET English 105, 106 Practice Test 1
    2. Study Guides   3. CSET   4. Teachers' Certification & Licensure
    5. Careers

Disclaimer:
The opinions expressed in this publication are the sole works of XAMonline and were created independently from the National Education Association, Educational Testing Service, or any State Department of Education, National Evaluation Systems or other testing affiliates.

Between the time of publication and printing, state specific standards as well as testing formats and website information may change that is not included in part or in whole within this product. Sample test questions are developed by XAMonline and reflect similar content as on real tests; however, they are not former tests. XAMonline assembles content that aligns with state standards but makes no claims nor guarantees teacher candidates a passing score. Numerical scores are determined by testing companies such as NES or ETS and then are compared with individual state standards. A passing score varies from state to state.

Printed in the United States of America   œ-1
CSET English 105, 106 Practice Test 1
ISBN: 978-1-60787-161-3

High School English
Pre-Test Sample Questions

1. When studying Shakespeare's play *Romeo and Juliet*, Becca was able to explain Juliet's feelings after she acted out a few scenes. What is Becca's learning style?
   (Average)

   A. Visual

   B. Verbal

   C. Aural

   D. Physical

2. While Will is reading a magazine article aloud to the class, he stops at a difficult passage and asks the teacher for clarification. What skill is Will developing?
   (Rigorous)

   A. Inferencing

   B. Summarizing

   C. Monitoring

   D. Paraphrasing

3. What is the main idea in this paragraph?
   (Easy)

   (1) English language learners (ELLs) may have some difficulty identifying the main idea when they are reading a paragraph. (2) Teaching students how to paraphrase can help them learn to pick out what is important in the material that they read. (3) This is a great strategy which you can accompany with other effective practices, such as previewing the story, making predictions, activating prior knowledge, using text features such as the title and other headings, and pre-reading key sections (like the introduction and conclusion). (4) All of these strategies will help ELLs improve their understanding of the material they are reading better as they identify the important points in the text, and the main idea.
   —Caryn Bachar, "Finding the Main Idea."
   http://www.colorincolorado.org/article/13349

   A. Sentence 1

   B. Sentence 2

   C. Sentence 3

   D. Sentence 4

4. Which of the following is an effective summary of this paragraph?
   (Rigorous)

   With technology providing a growing list of ways to communicate with each other, we sometimes lose sight of the significance of face-to-face communication. "Face-to-face communication remains the most powerful human interaction," says Kathleen Begley, Ed.D., author of *Face-to-Face Communication, Making Human Connections in a Technology-Driven World*. "As wonderful as electronic devices are, they can never fully replace the intimacy and immediacy of people conversing in the same room and it has worked for millions of years." Perhaps this explains the popularity of Starbucks and other places where associates and friends can get together to make a person-to-person connection.

   A. Experts agree that face-to-face communication is more effective than electronic communication

   B. People must learn to balance face-to-face communication with electronic communication

   C. Technology has replaced face-to-face communication

   D. Face-to-face communication provides a personal connection that is often lost through technology

5. In introducing the novella *The Things They Carried* by Tim O'Brien, Mr. Crown provides background information about the author's experiences in Vietnam and distributes an excerpt from one of O'Brien's short stories titled "How to Tell a True War Story." What is the method of text interpretation Mr. Crown is using?
   (Rigorous)

   A. Generating questions

   B. Determining the author's context

   C. Understanding symbols

   D. All of the above

6. Which of the following is not true about figurative language?
   (Average)

   A. Figurative language allows for deeper meaning than literal language

   B. Poets use figurative language to help readers see more clearly and focus on particulars

   C. Students should understand essential terminology of figurative language in order to analyze literature

   D. To prevent ambiguity, essayists avoid figurative language

7. What is the term for this quote?
   (Rigorous)

   "To err is human; to forgive is divine."
   —Alexander Pope

   A. Antithesis

   B. Synecdoche

   C. Aphorism

   D. Inversion

8. What figure of speech is used in this example?
   (Rigorous)

   Long time the manxome foe he sought. / So rested he by the Tumtum tree...
   —Lewis Carroll, "Jabberwocky

   A. Antithesis

   B. Synecdoche

   C. Inversion

   D. Conceit

9. The emotional attachment to a word is called
   (Easy)

   A. Connotation

   B. Denotation

   C. Definition

   D. Diction

10. What is the poetic structure of this example?
    (Rigorous)

    What dire offence from am'rous causes springs,
    What mighty contests rise from trivial things
    —Alexander Pope, lines 1 and 2, "The Rape of the Lock"

    A. Blank verse

    B. Heroic couplet

    C. Free verse

    D. Octava rima

11. **Which of these is not an example of personification?**
    (Rigorous)

    A. "The wind stood up and gave a shout. He whistled on his two fingers." —"The Wind" by James Stephens

    B. "Only the champion daisy trees were serene. After all, they were part of a rain forest already two thousand years old and scheduled for eternity, so they ignored the men and continued to rock the diamondbacks that slept in their arms. It took the river to persuade them that indeed the world was altered." —*Tar Baby* by Toni Morrison

    C. "I am silver and exact. I have no preconceptions/Whatever I see, I swallow immediately/Just as it is, unmisted by love or dislike./ I am not cruel, only truthful" —"Mirror" by Sylvia Plath

    D. "I heard a fly buzz when I died;/ The stillness round my form/Was like the stillness in the air/Between the heaves of storm." —"Dying" by Emily Dickinson

12. **In the O. Henry short story "The Gift of the Magi," the young husband sells his watch to buy hair combs for his wife and the young wife sells her hair to buy a watch fob for her husband. This is an example of**
    (Easy)

    A. Irony

    B. Parallelism

    C. Epiphany

    D. Stream of consciousness

13. **Which of the following is not true about plot?**
    (Average)

    A. One way to analyze plot is to note the action verbs

    B. Plot is the sequence of events in the story

    C. Character is a literary element that often propels the plot

    D. Plot is found only in fiction

14. What literary element is most noticeable in this excerpt from James Baldwin's *Sonny's Blues*? *(Easy)*

    When he was about as old as the boys in my class his face had been bright and open, there was a lot of copper in it; and he'd had wonderfully direct brown eyes, and great gentleness and privacy. I wonder what he looked like now. He had been picked up, the evening before, in a raid on an apartment downtown, for peddling and using heroin.

    A. Character

    B. Setting

    C. Plot

    D. Mood

15. What literary element is most noticeable in this excerpt from the short story "A Clean Well Lighted Place" by Ernest Hemingway? *(Average)*

    Turning off the electric light he continued the conversation with himself, it was the light of course but it is necessary that the place be clean and pleasant. You do not want music. Certainly you do not want music. Nor can you stand before a bar with dignity although that is all that is provided for these hours. What did he fear? It was not a fear or dread, it was a nothing that he knew too well. It was all a nothing and a man was a nothing too. It was only that and light was all it needed and a certain cleanness and order. Some lived in it and never felt it but he knew it all was nada y pues nada y nada y pues nada. Our nada who art in nada, nada be thy name thy kingdom nada thy will be nada in nada as it is in nada. Give us this nada our daily nada and nada us our nada as we nada our nadas and nada us not into nada but deliver us from nada; pues nada. Hail nothing full of nothing, nothing is with thee. He smiled and stood before a bar with a shining steam pressure coffee machine.

    A. Theme

    B. Character

    C. Mood

    D. Dialogue

16. Which of these would be an effective way to describe the theme of Shakespeare's *Romeo and Juliet*?
    (Average)

    A. Star-crossed lovers

    B. Family prejudices can cause grief and death

    C. Romantic love can be an overpowering force

    D. Love

17. In which genre did Tennessee Williams write?
    (Easy)

    A. Essays

    B. Drama

    C. Poetry

    D. Short Story

18. Which of the following is not a typical literary device used in drama?
    (Average)

    A. Aside

    B. Soliloquy

    C. Chorus

    D. Sermon

19. What type of literary work is non-fiction prose focusing on a topic and propounding a definite point of view and authoritative tone?
    (Easy)

    A. Epistle

    B. Essay

    C. Epic

    D. Allegory

20. Which of the following authors is not considered an essayist?
    (Average)

    A. Charles Lamb

    B. Ralph Waldo Emerson

    C. Michel de Montaigne

    D. Robert Browning

21. Which of the following can be called a fable?
    (Average)

    A. *Animal Farm* by George Orwell

    B. *Canterbury Tales* by Geoffrey Chaucer

    C. *Pride and Prejudice* by Jane Austen

    D. *Gulliver's Travels* by Jonathan Swift

22. **Which playwright changed the idea of the tragic hero to include the common man?**
    (Average)

    A. Arthur Miller

    B. Sophocles

    C. William Shakespeare

    D. Jean Racine

23. **On *The Rocky and Bullwinkle Show* cartoon show, dashing hero Dudley Do-Right of the Mounties saves the wholesome heroine Nell Fenwick who has been tied to the railroad tracks by the mean villain Snidely Whiplash. What type of comedy is this?**
    (Rigorous)

    A. Farce

    B. Burlesque

    C. Comic drama

    D. Melodrama

24. **What is the purpose of an octave in a Petrarchan sonnet?**
    (Rigorous)

    A. It states a problem, asks a question, or expresses an emotion

    B. It introduces the characters and sets the tone

    C. It resolves a problem, answers a question, or responds to an emotion

    D. It sets the mood and rhyme pattern for the rest of the poem

25. **Which type of sonnet uses the quatrain-and-couplet pattern with an abab bcbc cdcd ee rhyming pattern?**
    (Rigorous)

    A. The Spenserian sonnet

    B. The Petrarchan sonnet

    C. The English sonnet

    D. The Italian sonnet

26. Which type of sonnet is exemplified by the following?
    (Rigorous)

    What guyle is this, that those her golden tresses
    She doth attyre under a net of gold,
    And with sly skill so cunningly them dresses,
    That which is gold or haire may scarse be told?
    Is it that mens frayle eyes, which gaze too bold,
    She may entangle in that golden snare;
    And, being caught, may craftily enfold
    Their weaker harts, which are not wel aware?
    Take heed therefore, myne eyes, how ye doe stare
    Henceforth too rashly on that guilefull net,
    In which if ever ye entrapped are,
    Out of her bands ye by no meanes shall get.
    Fondnesse it were for any, being free,
    To covet fetters, though they golden bee!

    A. English sonnet

    B. Italian sonnet

    C. Spenserian sonnet

    D. Petrarchan sonnet

27. Which of the following is not a ballad?
    (Rigorous)

    A. "The Rime of the Ancient Mariner" by Samuel Taylor Coleridge

    B. "The Walrus and the Carpenter" by Lewis Carroll

    C. "Do Not Go Gentle Into That Good Night" by Dylan Thomas

    D. "La Belle Dame Sans Merci" by John Keats

28. Which of the following is not an allusion?
    (Average)

    A. After being on restriction for a week, John started calling his bedroom Elba

    B. Chocolate is my Achilles' heel

    C. You're tilting at windmills if you expect me to cooperate

    D. He served as peacemaker between the two foes

29. **Which type of literary genre encompasses fictional stories involving children or animals that come in contact with supernatural beings via magic?**
    (Easy)

    A. Fairy tales

    B. Myths

    C. Fables

    D. Folktales

30. **Which of the following is not a tall tale?**
    (Average)

    A. While traveling in a covered wagon, Pecos Bill fell out unnoticed by his family near the Pecos River and was raised by coyotes

    B. In "The Swollen Tree," a rattlesnake bites a tree, which swells so large that a hunter is able to build a five-room house from the wood

    C. In North Carolina, Bear Creek got its name from the season that Daniel Boone killed ninety-nine bears along its water

    D. To scratch an itch, Babe the Blue Ox would rub against a cliff

31. **Which genre of American Literature wrote about the common man and his socioeconomic problems in a non-sentimental way?**
    (Rigorous)

    A. Native American Literature

    B. Colonial Literature

    C. Romantic Literature

    D. Realistic Literature

32. **Whose writings from early American literature relate the hardships of crossing the Atlantic and the misery and suffering of the first colonists?**
    (Easy)

    A. Anne Bradstreet

    B. William Bradford

    C. William Byrd

    D. Thomas Paine

33. **Which of the following is a characteristic of literature during the Revolutionary Period?**
    (Average)

    A. Fiction, such as poems and novels

    B. Fiction, such as short stories and plays

    C. Non-fiction, such as essays, pamphlets, speeches, documents, and epistles

    D. Non-fiction, such as dictionaries, encyclopedias, and atlases

34. **Who was not considered one of the "Fireside Poets"?**
    (Average)

    A. Nathaniel Hawthorne

    B. James Russell Lowell

    C. Henry Wadsworth Longfellow

    D. John Greenleaf Whittier

35. **Which of the following is the story of an accident at sea that results in the death of one of the ship's officers, Claggert, a slug of a fellow who had taken a dislike to a young, affable, shy sailor. Captain Vere must hang the sailor for the death of Claggert but knows that his punishment is not just. However, an example must be given to the rest of the crew so that discipline can be maintained?**
    (Average)

    A. *Moby Dick*

    B. *Billy Budd*

    C. *The House of Seven Gables*

    D. "On the Duty of Civil Disobedience"

36. **Identify the style/period of this poem?**
    (Rigorous)

    It was many and many a year ago,
    In a kingdom by the sea,
    That a maiden there lived whom you may know
    By the name of Annabel Lee;
    And this maiden she lived with no other thought
    Than to love and be loved by me.

    A. Neoclassicism

    B. Romanticism

    C. Realism

    D. Naturalism

37. Who is the author of this poem?
    (Easy)

    Because I could not stop for Death,
    He kindly stopped for me;
    The carriage held but just ourselves
    And Immortality.
    We slowly drove, he knew no haste,
    And I had put away
    My labor, and my leisure too,
    For his civility.

    A. Emily Dickinson

    B. John Greenleaf Whittier

    C. Walt Whitman

    D. James Lowell

38. Which of these was written during the Medieval Period of British Literature?
    (Average)

    A. *Beowulf*

    B. *Le Morte d'Arthur*

    C. *Samson Agonistes*

    D. *The Rape of the Lock*

39. In what period of British literature was this verse written?
    (Rigorous)

    From fairest creatures we desire increase,
    That thereby beauty's rose might never die,
    But as the riper should by time decease,
    His tender heir might bear his memory:
    But thou, contracted to thine own bright eyes,
    Feed'st thy light's flame with self-substantial fuel,
    Making a famine where abundance lies,
    Thyself thy foe, to thy sweet self too cruel.
    Thou that art now the world's fresh ornament
    And only herald to the gaudy spring,
    Within thine own bud buriest thy content
    And, tender churl, makest waste in niggarding.
    Pity the world, or else this glutton be,
    To eat the world's due, by the grave and thee.

    A. Anglo-Saxon Period

    B. Medieval Period

    C. Renaissance Period

    D. Seventeenth century

40. Identify the period of British Literature for this excerpt.
    (Average)

    No man is an island,
    Entire of itself.
    Each is a piece of the continent,
    A part of the main.
    If a clod be washed away by the sea,
    Europe is the less.
    As well as if a promontory were.
    As well as if a manner of thine own
    Or of thine friend's were.
    Each man's death diminishes me,
    For I am involved in mankind.
    Therefore, send not to know
    For whom the bell tolls,
    It tolls for thee.

    A. Renaissance

    B. Seventeenth century

    C. Eighteenth century

    D. Nineteenth century

41. Which of the following were not authors during the Enlightenment of the eighteenth century?
    (Average)

    A. Alexander Pope

    B. Daniel Defoe

    C. James Boswell

    D. William Blake

42. Which of these authors did not write during the British Romantic Period of the nineteenth century?
    (Rigorous)

    A. George Eliot

    B. Jane Austen

    C. Alfred, Lord Tennyson

    D. Charlotte Bronte

43. Which of the following is not a characteristic of the Pre-Raphaelites?
    (Rigorous)

    A. Reacted against Victorian materialism

    B. Affirmed the neoclassical conventions of academic art

    C. Produced earnest, quasi-religious works

    D. Encouraged artists and writers to practice each other's art

44. Which of the following was not a dramatist of the twentieth century?
    (Easy)

    A. George Bernard Shaw

    B. Arthur Miller

    C. Tom Stoppard

    D. Henrik Ibsen

45. **Which of the following French authors has not won the Nobel Prize for Literature?**
    (Rigorous)

    A. Albert Camus

    B. Eugene Ionesco

    C. Jean-Paul Sartre

    D. Samuel Beckett

46. **What changed occurred in adolescent literature in the seventeenth century?**
    (Average)

    A. Literature began to be written specifically for the young

    B. The Puritans in Europe were able to ban all literature aimed at children

    C. Publishers began to offer large stipends to authors of children's literature

    D. More authors began to write long novels for young readers

47. **Children's literature that functions at the concrete operations stage, focuses on the "good person," has plots dependent on external rewards, and exhibits all five needs from Maslow's hierarchy is appropriate for what reading level?**
    (Rigorous)

    A. Fifth and Sixth Grades

    B. Seventh and Eighth Grades

    C. Ninth Grade

    D. Tenth to Twelfth Grade

48. **Which of the following is not a challenge in selecting books at the appropriate reading level?**
    (Average)

    A. The diverse interests of students

    B. The diverse reading levels of students

    C. The availability of realistic fiction

    D. The lack of high-interest books for on- or below-level readers

49. **Which of the following works deal with the subject of immigration?**
    (Average)

    A. *Uncle Tom's Cabin*

    B. *The Joy Luck Club*

    C. *Go Tell It on the Mountain*

    D. *Catch-22*

50. Which period of literature is patterned after the writings of Greeks and Romans, does not exalt the self, and focuses on the group rather than the individual?
(Easy)

   A. Neoclassicism

   B. Romanticism

   C. Realism

   D. Naturalism

51. Which of the following is not a member of the first generation of Romantic writers?
(Rigorous)

   A. William Wordsworth

   B. Samuel Taylor Coleridge

   C. Ralph Waldo Emerson

   D. Percy Bysshe Shelley

52. Which term can be defined as words or sentences that help readers determine the meanings of words?
(Easy)

   A. Prior knowledge.

   B. Context clues.

   C. Comprehension.

   D. Cues.

53. In an essay on "The Cask of the Amontillado," Jorge writes this sentence: "This short story by Poe is not his best example of horror fiction. I prefer 'The Tell-Tale Heart' because of the way the author builds suspense and adds tension throughout the story." Which type of reading response does this illustrate?
(Rigorous)

   A. Emotional

   B. Interpretive

   C. Critical

   D. Evaluative

54. In her AP English class, Miriam has written an essay comparing and contrasting the works of John Steinbeck as they reflect the social and economic times of the first half of the twentieth century. What type of literary response does this represent?
(Rigorous)

   A. Emotional

   B. Interpretive

   C. Critical

   D. Evaluative

55. What is the SQ3R method of reading comprehension?
    (Average)

    A. Study, Quiz, Recite, Review, Remember

    B. Survey, Question, Read, Recite, Recognize

    C. Survey, Question, Read, Recite, Review

    D. Summarize, Question, Read, Recall, Review

56. Ms. Prince is reading and scoring portfolios that students submitted after their study of Romeo and Juliet. What is the correct term for this process?
    (Rigorous)

    A. Evaluation

    B. Planning

    C. Assessment

    D. Interpretation

57. After Mr. Whitson's class has left, he writes brief comments about each student's participation in discussion for that day. What type of assessment is this?
    (Average)

    A. Formal

    B. Informal

    C. Holistic

    D. Formative

Direction: Read this poem and answer questions 58–62:

Out, Out—

The buzz-saw snarled and rattled in the yard
And made dust and dropped stove-length sticks of wood,
Sweet-scented stuff when the breeze drew across it.
And from there those that lifted eyes could count
Five mountain ranges one behind the other
Under the sunset far into Vermont.
And the saw snarled and rattled, snarled and rattled,
As it ran light, or had to bear a load.
And nothing happened: day was all but done.
Call it a day, I wish they might have said
To please the boy by giving him the half hour
That a boy counts so much when saved from work.
His sister stood beside them in her apron
To tell them "Supper." At the word, the saw,
As if to prove saws knew what supper meant,
Leaped out at the boy's hand, or seemed to leap—
He must have given the hand. However it was,
Neither refused the meeting. But the hand!
The boy's first outcry was a rueful laugh.
As he swung toward them holding up the hand
Half in appeal, but half as if to keep
The life from spilling. Then the boy saw all—
Since he was old enough to know, big boy
Doing a man's work, though a child at heart—
He saw all spoiled. "Don't let him cut my hand off—
The doctor, when he comes. Don't let him, sister!"
So. But the hand was gone already.
The doctor put him in the dark of ether.
He lay and puffed his lips out with his breath.
And then—the watcher at his pulse took fright.
No one believed. They listened at his heart.
Little—less—nothing! —and that ended it.
No more to build on there. And they, since they
Were not the one dead, turned to their affairs.

—Robert Frost

58. **Identify the figure of speech in the first line of the poem "The buzz-saw snarled and rattled in the yard"?**
    (Easy)

    A. Assonance

    B. Onomatopoeia

    C. Apostrophe

    D. Metaphor

59. **Identify the figure of speech in this line: "So. But the hand was gone already."**
    (Rigorous)

    A. Metonymy

    B. Allusion

    C. Personification

    D. Synecdoche

60. **What type of poetry is "Out, Out—"?**
    (Average)

    A. Narrative

    B. Dramatic

    C. Epic

    D. Lyric

61. **What literary element is represented by the poem's title "Out, Out—"?**
    (Rigorous)

    A. Oxymoron

    B. Personification

    C. Onomatopoeia

    D. Literary allusion

62. **Which of the following would be an interpretive question to ask students about this poem?**
    (Rigorous)

    A. How does Frost make the buzz-saw look sinister?

    B. How do you feel about apparent indifference of the people in the last two lines?

    C. Compare this poem to "Sir Patrick Spence," a traditional Scottish ballad. How do these poems represent narrative poetry?

    D. Does Frost's poem effectively convey the theme of the effect of a meaningless death?

Directions: Read this poem and answer questions 63–67.

The Lake Isle of Innisfree

I will arise and go now, and go to Innisfree,
And a small cabin build there, of clay and wattles made:
Nine bean-rows will I have there, a hive for the honey-bee;
And live alone in the bee-loud glade.

And I shall have some peace there, for peace comes dropping slow,
Dropping from the veils of the morning to where the cricket sings;
There midnight's all a glimmer, and noon a purple glow,
And evening full of the linnet's wings.

I will arise and go now, for always night and day
I hear lake water lapping with low sounds by the shore;
While I stand on the roadway, or on the pavements grey,
I hear it in the deep heart's core.
—William Butler Yeats

63. What literary element is used in the line "I hear lake water lapping with low sounds by the shore"? *(Easy)*

   A. Alliteration

   B. Caesura

   C. Assonance

   D. Sprung rhythm

64. What type of poetry is "The Lake Isle of Innisfree"? *(Rigorous)*

   A. Dramatic

   B. Narrative

   C. Epic

   D. Lyric

65. What literary element is represented by the poem's lines: "Nine bean-rows will I have there, a hive for the honey-bee/And live alone in the bee-loud glade. *(Rigorous)*

   A. Literary allusion

   B. Personification

   C. Onomatopoeia

   D. Oxymoron

66. Which of the following would be an evaluative question to ask students about this poem? *(Rigorous)*

    A. Does reading "The Lake Isle of Innisfree" remind you of any places you have been?

    B. Does Yeats achieve his purpose in conveying the picture of the lake isle?

    C. How is Yeats' poem an example of lyric poetry of the Victorian period?

    D. How does the diction of Yeats contribute to the musical quality of the poem?

67. How can students determine the meaning of the word "wattles"? *(Average)*

    A. Using context clues of the preceding phrase "And a small cabin build there, of clay and wattle made" students can understand that it is a building material

    B. Using prior knowledge, students will draw on their past experiences in nature and realize that it is something like clay

    C. Using connotation, students will understand this it is a positive word

    D. Using the poet's explanation in the next line with the phrase "nine bean-rows, students will understand that it is a type of plant

68. Which of the following is not an internal factor affecting Juan's language development? *(Rigorous)*

    A. Juan celebrates his 8th birthday

    B. Juan had ear infections as a baby

    C. Juan is the youngest of four children

    D. Juan experienced developmental delays after a premature birth

69. Which approach of language development is based on the idea that language ability is innate and develops through natural human maturation?
   (Easy)

   A. Learning approach

   B. Linguistic approach

   C. Cognitive approach

   D. Sociocognitive approach

70. Which of the following would be an effective way to incorporate the sociocognitive approach to learning development in a classroom?
   (Average)

   A. Provide opportunities for students to make oral presentations

   B. Encourage students to engage in silent reading

   C. Provide individualized online research activities

   D. Encourage students to keep journals

71. Ian drives a lorry through the streets of London, takes a lift to his second-floor flat, and eats bangers and mash for dinner. Maia drives a truck in Boston, uses the elevator to get to her fifth-floor apartment, and cooks hot dogs for dinner. What language influences are demonstrated by this scenario?
   (Average)

   A. Social

   B. Personal

   C. Geographical

   D. Genetic

72. **Which of the following is written in Middle English?**
    (Rigorous)

    A. HWÆT, WE GAR-DEna in geardagum,Þeodcyni nga þrym gefrunon,hu ða æþelingas ellen fremedon!

    B. But for to tellen yow of his array,His hors were goode, but he was nat gay.Of fustian he wered a gyponAl bismotered with his habergeon,For he was late ycome from his viage,And wente for to doon his pilgrymage.

    C. To be, or not to be: that is the question:Whether 'tis nobler in the mind to sufferThe slings and arrows of outrageous fortune,Or to take arms against a sea of troubles,And by opposing end them?

    D. I have been assured by a very knowing American of my acquaintance in London, that a young healthy child well nursed is at a year old a most delicious, nourishing, and wholesome food, whether stewed, roasted, baked, or boiled.

73. **Which of the following is not true about the growth of the English language?**
    (Rigorous)

    A. Spanish and English colonization contributed to the growth of English in Western hemisphere

    B. Modern inventions such as radios, television, and movies have helped to standardize pronunciation

    C. Technology has expanded English vocabulary

    D. English is easier to learn because of its rules and structure

74. **In what way is the English language slower to change?**
    (Rigorous)

    A. Spelling

    B. Vocabulary

    C. Pronunciation

    D. Syntax

75. **What three parts can form a word?**
    (Average Rigor)

    A. A prefix, a neologism, and a syllable.

    B. A root word, a suffix, and a syllable.

    C. A syllable, a neologism, and a suffix.

    D. A prefix, a root word, and a suffix.

76. **In the word "absenteeism," what does the suffix "ism" mean?**
    (Rigorous)

    A. Resembling

    B. The act of

    C. Capable of

    D. The study of

77. **What is the definition of vernacular?**
    (Average)

    A. The history of a word

    B. A new word or phrase added to the vocabulary

    C. The language of a particular group or region

    D. An informal word or phrase used by a particular group

78. **Which of the following is not true about spelling?**
    (Rigorous)

    A. English spelling is complicated because it does not follow the one-sound, one letter formula

    B. English spelling became easier with more phonetic representation of sounds

    C. The English adopted the Latin-based alphabet with changes from the Greeks and Romans

    D. English spelling became more standardized after the invention of the printing press

79. **Which of the following is a compound sentence?**
    (Average)

    A. Neither Laurie nor Billy trusted the accountant with their tax return.

    B. Although Shakespeare wrote in Modern English, high school students will have a difficult time with the language.

    C. Spellcheckers can be your first line of defense against spelling errors and typos, but they are not infallible.

    D. Vivi and Kasi offered to help but left before the meeting was over.

80. **Which sentence uses subordination to show condition?**
    (Rigorous)

    A. Because a database lists thousands of records, you must develop an effective search strategy.

    B. Whether you consider yourself a good or bad speller, you must take time to proofread.

    C. Although your friends might understand jargon, you should use concrete terms to write business letters.

    D. Unless you object, we will proceed.

81. **Which of the following sentences has a dangling modifier?**
    (Rigorous)

    A. Having worked sixty hours last week, John refused to work on Saturday.

    B. To stay in touch with parents, telephone contacts are necessary.

    C. If anyone has a cell phone, turn it off now.

    D. After calling the faculty together, the principal announced her retirement this year.

82. **Which of the following sentences has an error in parallel structure?**
    (Rigorous)

    A. Colleen ate the ice cream with enthusiasm and in a hurry.

    B. After hiking for hours, Joe sat down to rest and drink water.

    C. Ms. Hill is expected to teach five sections, to counsel students, and to prepare lesson plans.

    D. The book was exciting, well written, and it interested me.

83. **Choose the sentence in active voice.**
    (Average)

    A. Your vacation request is approved, pending my signature.

    B. Rain and slick road conditions caused the accident.

    C. The assignment must be submitted by the end of the week.

    D. Mrs. Johnson's automobile was inspected by the insurance company.

84. **Identify the sentence that is capitalized correctly.**
    (Easy)

    A. Both my Father and Uncle John went fishing at the Washington dike last Thursday.

    B. Because Labor Day is a federal holiday, all banks will be closed.

    C. During the Spring Semester, the students from Washington academy made plans for the fall 2010 student orientation program.

    D. The Late President Lyndon Johnson, who served in Office during the civil rights era, is remembered for his policies on integration.

85. **What prewriting strategy is used to write down whatever comes to mind?**
    (Easy)

    A. Free writing

    B. Revising

    C. Editing

    D. Publishing

86. **What term is used in making a list of all ideas connected with your topic?**
    (Easy)

    A. Brainstorming

    B. Inspiration

    C. Breakthrough

    D. Innovation

87. **Which of these is part of the editing stage?**
    (Average)

    A. Proofread the draft for punctuation and mechanical errors

    B. Use computer programs to check grammar and spelling

    C. Share papers with peers

    D. All of the above

88. **Which of these errors would be caught by a spellchecker?**
    (Average)

    A. The decision was left up to he and I.

    B. Tuan used the vaccuum cleaner to clean out the car.

    C. Spellcheckers is useful for proofreading.

    D. The Norman Conquest was in 1966.

89. Which of the following is not a technique for creating a supportive classroom environment?
(Average)

   A. Provide several prompts or give students the freedom to write on a topic of their choice

   B. Respond to oral queries with a question whenever possible. Your response should be non-critical. Use positive, supportive language

   C. Create peer response/support groups that work on dissimilar writing assignments.

   D. Provide the group with a series of questions to guide them through the group writing sessions.

90. When assessing and responding to student writing, which guideline is not formative?
(Rigorous)

   A. Reread the writing and note at the end whether the student met the objective of the writing task

   B. Responses should be non-critical and should use supportive and encouraging language

   C. Explain the criteria that will be used for assessment in advance

   D. For the first reading, use a holistic method, examining the work as a whole

91. What steps should you follow in gathering your data or information?
(Average)

   A. Keep a record of any sources consulted during the research process

   B. As you take notes, avoid unintentional plagiarism

   C. Summarize and paraphrase in your own words without the source in front of you

   D. All of the above

92. Which of the following resources is the beginning point for many research projects?
(Average)

   A. Encyclopedias

   B. Dictionaries

   C. Databases

   D. The Internet

93. When searching online databases for information about the amount of money spent on bilingual education in private schools, which Boolean operators will generate the smallest number of hits?
    (Rigorous)

    A. "bilingual education" not "private schools"

    B. "bilingual education" and "private schools"

    C. "bilingual education" or "private schools"

    D. "bilingual educat*" or "private schools"

94. Which of the following materials are not considered a primary source?
    (Average)

    A. Literature and nonverbal materials, novels, stories, poetry, and essays from the period, as well as coins, archaeological artifacts, and art produced during the period

    B. Documents that reflect the immediate, everyday concerns of people: memoranda, bills, deeds, charters, newspaper reports, pamphlets, graffiti, popular writings, journals or diaries, records of decision-making bodies, letters, receipts, snapshots, and so on

    C. Books written on the basis of primary materials about the period of time

    D. Narrative accounts of events, ideas, and trends written with intentionality by someone contemporary with the events described

95. Dr. Alvin in thinking about buying a new car wants to research the following criteria: comfort, safety, and affordability. Which of the following would not qualify as primary research?
    (Rigorous)

    A. He visits a local dealership and test drives the latest model

    B. He picks up product brochures and creates a spreadsheet comparing and contrasting different models

    C. He visits Edmunds.com to check customer reviews

    D. He reads an article in Car and Driver that rates vehicles based on independent tests

96. Which of the following criteria would not be useful in determining the credibility of information found on a website?
    (Average)

    A. Accuracy

    B. Timeliness

    C. Source

    D. Ease of use

97. What is another name for in-text documentation?
    (Average)

    A. Parenthetical documentation

    B. Footnotes

    C. Works Consulted

    D. Bibliography

98. Which of the following is a correct bibliographic citation based on MLA style?
    (Average)

    A. Wynne, Sharon. *English Language, Literature, and Composition: Teacher Certification Exam*. Boston: XAMOnline, Inc., 2010.

    B. Sharon Wynne. *English Language, Literature, and Composition: Teacher Certification Exam*. Boston: XAMOnline, Inc., 2010.

    C. Wynne, Sharon. (2010) *English language, literature, and composition: teacher certification exam*. Boston: XAMOnline, Inc.

    D. Sharon Wynne, "English Language, Literature, and Composition: Teacher Certification Exam." Boston: XAMOnline, Inc., 2010.

99. Which of the following would require a formal level of language?
    (Average)

    A. A letter to the editor of the newspaper expressing appreciation for the police protection of a neighborhood event

    B. A report to the school board detailing the school's plan to improve the dropout rate of minority students

    C. A letter to the parents of students announcing the opening of the new school library

    D. A cover letter to the principal of a school requesting a job interview

100. Which of the following are students assessing about their audience when they ask these questions: What is important to this group of people, what is their background, and how will that background affect their perception of your writing?
     (Rigorous)

     A. Constraints

     B. Needs

     C. Values

     D. Demographics

101. What are the three basic principles to follow to be convincing in writing or speaking?
     (Average)

     A. Emphasis, transition, and unity

     B. Coherence, emphasis, and transition

     C. Unity, coherence, and transition

     D. Unity, coherence, and emphasis

102. Which of the following would be an effective topic sentence to unify this paragraph?
    (Rigorous)

    Club Palm Resort's beaches are beautiful, and the surrounding countryside is quite scenic. The quality of the food leaves a lot to be desired. Many vacationers enjoy the variety of outdoor activities and the instruction available in such sports as sailing and scuba diving. Unfortunately, security is poor; several vacationers' rooms have been broken into and their valuables stolen. Christmas in the Bahamas can make the thought of New Year's in Chicago bearable.

    A. Vacationers should take advantage of warmer climes for midwinter holidays.

    B. A vacation at Club Palm Resort has its good points and bad points.

    C. Club Palm Resort's isolation created dissatisfaction among some vacationers.

    D. For vacationers sick and tired of the frozen north, a week at Club Palm Resort can provide just the midwinter thaw they need.

103. What is the structural problem with this paragraph?
    (Average)

    Club Palm Resort's isolation created dissatisfaction among some vacationers. The quality of the food was poor. People want a choice of entertainment in the evening. Most of us spent too much time together day after day. People expect to be able to go out for a meal if they feel like it.

    A. Development

    B. Coherence

    C. Unity

    D. Transition

104. Which of the following sentences uses transition to show contrasting ideas?
    (Average)

    A. In order to make the deadline, I will need to work throughout the weekend.

    B. The camping trip was postponed because of bad weather; obviously, the scouts were very disappointed.

    C. Americans are proud of their traditions, yet they are not afraid of new ideas.

    D. Before Dana could attend the street fair, she needed to complete her literature essay on the poetry of Emily Dickinson.

105. Which of the following is a disadvantage of a graphic message?
(*Average*)

   A. Gives a quick overview of some quantifiable situation

   B. Conveys a much shorter range of information

   C. Relies on the ability of the viewer to understand the information

   D. Provides visual appeal

106. Which type of written discourse implies the writer's ability to select vocabulary and arrange facts and opinions in such a way as to direct the actions of the listener/reader?
(*Average*)

   A. Persuasive writing

   B. Descriptive writing

   C. Narrative writing

   D. Basic expository writing

107. Which communication technique usually helps the speaker overcome speech anxiety by connecting with the attentive audience and easing feelings of isolation?
(*Easy*)

   A. Eye contact

   B. Gestures

   C. Movement

   D. Voice

108. What refers to the emotional appeal made by the speaker to the listener and emphasizes the fact that an audience responds to ideas with emotion?
(*Easy*)

   A. Pathos

   B. Logos

   C. Ethos

   D. Culture

109. In 1959, Volkswagen ran an advertising campaign with the motto "Think Small." What type of advertising technique does this represent?
(Rigorous)

   A. Compliment the consumer

   B. Escape

   C. Rebel

   D. Statistical claim

110. Which of the following is an example of inductive reasoning?
(Rigorous)

   A. Maria speaks Spanish and English; Jacques speaks French and English; Vlad speaks Russian and English. Therefore all students in my class are bilingual

   B. During the evening of September 3, Professor Plum was murdered in the library with the candlestick; Mrs. White saw Colonel Mustard leave the library that night with blood on his shoes; therefore Colonel Mustard was the murderer.

   C. Tom's American-made Ford Escort is green. Dick's American-made Chevy Volt is green; Harry's American-made Dodge viper is green; therefore, all American-made cars are green

   D. All of the students in my class are bilingual; Blake is a student in my class. Therefore Blake is bilingual

111. Which of the following is an example of a post hoc fallacy?
(Rigorous)

   A. When Simone sneezed, the tardy bell rang; therefore Simone caused the bell to ring

   B. Liz's computer crashed after she installed the new software; therefore, the software caused the computer crash

   C. When leaving the parking lot, Steve ran over some broken glass; on the way home, he got a flat tire; Steve reasons that the broken class caused his flat tire

   D. Cameron doesn't like to use Facebook; e joins the computer club and notes that everyone uses Facebook; the club president ridicules others for not using the social networking site; Cameron decides to set up a Facebook page

112. Which of the following is not written in first person point of view?
(Rigorous)

   A. *The Catcher in the Rye*

   B. *To Kill a Mockingbird*

   C. *The Great Gatsby*

   D. *The Old Man and the Sea*

113. Based on this brief excerpt from the short story "Miss Brill" by Katherine Mansfield, identify the point of view.
(Average)

Although it was so brilliantly fine—the blue sky powdered with gold and great spots of light like white wine splashed over the Jardins Publiques—Miss Brill was glad that she had decided on her fur. The air was motionless, but when you opened your mouth there was just a faint chill, like a chill from a glass of iced water before you sip, and now and again a leaf came drifting—from nowhere, from the sky. Miss Brill put up her hand and touched her fur. Dear little thing! It was nice to feel it again. She had taken it out of its box that afternoon, shaken out the moth-powder, given it a good brush, and rubbed the life back into the dim little eyes.

A. First person

B. Second person

C. Third person limited

D. Third person omniscient

114. What are decisions or declarations based on observations or reasoning that express approval or disapproval?
(Average)

A. Judgments

B. Facts

C. Opinions

D. Conclusions

115. In a job interview, Colleen, a recent graduate, explains how proud she is that she worked twenty hours a week while attending college and still maintained a 3.2 GPA. She voices her disdain about other graduates who had no outside jobs and earned lower GPAs. Which form of bias is seen in this example?
(Rigorous)

A. Cultural bias

B. Racial bias

C. Professional bias

D. Unconscious bias

Directions: Read the following essay and answer question 116:

The Insecure Sense of Femininity of Elisa
in John Steinbeck's Short Story "The Chrysanthemums

(1) John Steinbeck's' short story "The Chrysanthemums," narrates an everyday series of events, but the emotional drama that Elisa goes through is very significant. (2) Elisa thinks of herself as strong, but she is, in fact, a very vulnerable woman. (3) She may be vital enough to have strong ambitions, but she is so insecure about her own femininity that she is finally unable to cope with the strain of transforming her life. (4) When we first see Elisa we get an immediate sense that she is hiding her sexuality from the rest of the world. (5) The speed and energy with which Elisa later seeks to transform herself really bring out the extent of her dissatisfaction with the role she has been playing. (6) But Elisa's new sense of herself does not last, for she has insufficient inner strength to develop into the mature, independent woman she would like to be.

116. Which sentence expresses the conclusion?
(Average)

A. Sentence 1

B. Sentence 3

C. Sentence 5

D. Sentence 6

Directions: Read this paragraph and answer questions 117–120.

The argument that we need capital punishment in order to reduce the cost of maintaining the penal system is quite misplaced. There is no evidence that executing murderers will save us money. A number of studies of this question have shown that, on average, it costs about $50,000 per year to keep a maximum security offender in jail (Schneider, 2000; Ross and Sinclair 2006). A person who serves, say, a 25-year sentence, therefore, costs the state about $1,250,000. However, in countries which show some concern about the rights of the accused to a full and fair process, a system which has capital punishment for murder requires far more elaborate trials and a much lengthier and more expensive appeal process for capital offences than for non-capital offences. In addition, the cost of the execution itself is not insignificant. Recent studies by Gardner (2008) have shown that in the United States the cost of the various judicial processes and of the execution for convicted murderers is up to 30 percent higher than the cost of keeping them in jail for life. Other similar studies by McIntyre (2000) and Jackson (2005) have come to the same conclusion. There is, in other words, compelling reason seriously to question one of the most frequent claims made in support of capital punishment: that it will reduce costs significantly. In fact, if saving money is the main concern in the penal system, we should get rid of capital punishment immediately. *

*This text, which has been prepared by Ian Johnston of Malaspina University-College, Nanaimo, BC, is in the public domain and may be used, in whole or in part, without permission and without charge, released May 2000. [Ed. note: Sources are fictional and dates have been changed.]

117. **What type of appeal is used in this paragraph?**
(Rigorous)

   A. Logos

   B. Ethos

   C. Pathos

   D. Both logos and ethos

118. **In the essay on capital punishment, what is the purpose of the following sentence in the classical argument structure?**
(Average)

   There is no evidence that executing murderers will save us money.

   A. Narration

   B. Confirmation

   C. Refutation

   D. Summation

119. **In the essay on capital punishment, which of these sentences provides an effective summation?**
(Rigorous)

   A. In addition, the cost of the execution itself is not insignificant.

   B. There is, in other words, compelling reason seriously to question one of the most frequent claims made in support of capital punishment: that it will reduce costs significantly.

   C. In fact, if saving money is the main concern in the penal system, we should get rid of capital punishment immediately.

   D. Recent studies by Gardner (1998) have shown that in the United States the cost of the various judicial processes and of the execution for convicted murderers is up to 30 percent higher than the cost of keeping them in jail for life.

120. In the essay on capital punishment, what is the type of reasoning used?
(Average)

A. Deductive

B. Inductive

Praxis English Language, Literature, and Composition 0041
Pre-Test Sample Questions with Rationales

1. When studying Shakespeare's play *Romeo and Juliet*, Becca was able to explain Juliet's feelings after she acted out a few scenes. What is Becca's learning style?
   (Average)

    A. Visual

    B. Verbal

    C. Aural

    D. Physical

Answer: D. Physical
By using physical activity, Becca has shown that she is a kinesthetic learner and functions better with physicality. With a visual learning style, a learner understands better through pictures, charts, and video clips. With a verbal learning style, a learner understands through reading and vocabulary. With an aural learning style, a learner has stronger auditory skills and learns through listening as in verbal discussions.

2. While Will is reading a magazine article aloud to the class, he stops at a difficult passage and asks the teacher for clarification. What skill is Will developing?
   (Rigorous)

    A. Inferencing

    B. Summarizing

    C. Monitoring

    D. Paraphrasing

Answer: C. Monitoring
Monitoring is a process that students use to stop and think about what they are examining to clarify understanding. Inferencing is a process in which the reader makes a reasonable judgment based on the information given. Summarizing is examining the details of a longer passage or excerpt to determine the main idea. Paraphrasing is a more detailed form of summarizing and follows the chronology of the original piece.

3. What is the main idea in this paragraph?
   (Easy)

   (1) English language learners (ELLs) may have some difficulty identifying the main idea when they are reading a paragraph. (2) Teaching students how to paraphrase can help them learn to pick out what is important in the material that they read. (3) This is a great strategy which you can accompany with other effective practices, such as previewing the story, making predictions, activating prior knowledge, using text features such as the title and other headings, and pre-reading key sections (like the introduction and conclusion). (4) All of these strategies will help ELLs improve their understanding of the material they are reading better as they identify the important points in the text, and the main idea.
   —Caryn Bachar, "Finding the Main Idea."
   http://www.colorincolorado.org/article/13349

   A. Sentence 1

   B. Sentence 2

   C. Sentence 3

   D. Sentence 4

Answer: D. Sentence 4
Sentence 4 expresses the main idea by summarizing the preceding information. This sentence proves that main ideas can appear anywhere in a paragraph—and can even be implied. Sentence 1 provides a broad statement. Sentences 2 and 3 identify strategies to help ELL students.

4. Which of the following is an effective summary of this paragraph? (Rigorous)

With technology providing a growing list of ways to communicate with each other, we sometimes lose sight of the significance of face-to-face communication. "Face-to-face communication remains the most powerful human interaction," says Kathleen Begley, Ed.D., author of *Face-to-Face Communication, Making Human Connections in a Technology-Driven World*. "As wonderful as electronic devices are, they can never fully replace the intimacy and immediacy of people conversing in the same room and it has worked for millions of years." Perhaps this explains the popularity of Starbucks and other places where associates and friends can get together to make a person-to-person connection.

- A. Experts agree that face-to-face communication is more effective than electronic communication
- B. People must learn to balance face-to-face communication with electronic communication
- C. Technology has replaced face-to-face communication
- D. Face-to-face communication provides a personal connection that is often lost through technology

Answer: D. Face-to-face communication provides a personal connection that is often lost through technology

A summary is a brief restatement of the main idea. In this paragraph, the writer compares face-to-face communication with electronic communication and uses an outside source to support the main idea that "Face-to-face communication provides a personal connection that is often lost through technology." Choice A is incorrect because the original excerpt cites only one outside source and does contend that one communication style is more effective than another. Choice B is incorrect because the writer does not draw the conclusion that balance is necessary. Choice C is incorrect because there is no detail in the excerpt to support it.

5. In introducing the novella *The Things They Carried* by Tim O'Brien, Mr. Crown provides background information about the author's experiences in Vietnam and distributes an excerpt from one of O'Brien's short stories titled "How to Tell a True War Story." What is the method of text interpretation Mr. Crown is using?
    (Rigorous)

    A. Generating questions

    B. Determining the author's context

    C. Understanding symbols

    D. All of the above

Answer: B. Determining the author's context
Determining the author's context entails examining the author's feelings, beliefs, past experiences, goals, needs, and physical environment as suggested by the prose. Readers' experiences will be enriched if they can appreciate and understand how these elements may have affected the writing.

6. Which of the following is not true about figurative language?
    (Average)

    A. Figurative language allows for deeper meaning than literal language

    B. Poets use figurative language to help readers see more clearly and focus on particulars

    C. Students should understand essential terminology of figurative language in order to analyze literature

    D. To prevent ambiguity, essayists avoid figurative language

Answer: D. To prevent ambiguity, essayists avoid figurative language
All writers, whether of fiction or non-fiction, use figurative language. While some may do so more than others—poets in particular—figures of speech add layers to meaning. All the other statements are true.

7. **What is the term for this quote?**
   (Rigorous)

   "To err is human; to forgive is divine."
   —Alexander Pope

   A. Antithesis

   B. Synecdoche

   C. Aphorism

   D. Inversion

Answer: A. Antithesis
This line from Pope's "Essay on Criticism" is an example of antithesis, which is balanced writing about conflicting ideas. A synecdoche uses a word for a part of something to mean a whole. An aphorism is a short, often witty statement, presenting an observation or a universal truth; an adage. In inversion, the author rearranges the order of words to achieve an effect, such as Yoda in the Star Wars movie "To a dark place this line of thought will carry us" or "Obi-Wan, my choice is."

8. **What figure of speech is used in this example?**
   (Rigorous)

   Long time the manxome foe he sought. / So rested he by the Tumtum tree...
   —Lewis Carroll, "Jabberwocky"

   A. Antithesis

   B. Synecdoche

   C. Inversion

   D. Conceit

Answer: C. Inversion
This example uses inversion, because the author rearranges the order of words to achieve an effect. In the case of poetry, it is often to maintain rhythm or rhyme. Antithesis expresses conflicting ideas in a balanced syntactical structure. Synecdoche uses a part to represent a whole, as in the phrase "all hands on deck." A conceit is an extended metaphor as in the Shakespearean sonnet "Shall I compare thee to a summer day."

9. **The emotional attachment to a word is called**
   (Easy)

   A.   Connotation

   B.   Denotation

   C.   Definition

   D.   Diction

Answer: A. Connotation
Connotation is the idea or meaning suggested by or associated with a word or thing. Denotation is the literal definition of a word. Definition is the literal meaning of the word. Diction refers to the writer's style and is achieved by the choice and arrangement of words. For example, "house" can be defined as a structure in which people live. This is its denotation. "Mansion" and "shacks" are also structures in which people live and while they share the same definition, they have different connotations of size and cost.

10. **What is the poetic structure of this example?**
    (Rigorous)

    **What dire offence from am'rous causes springs,
    What mighty contests rise from trivial things**
    —Alexander Pope, lines 1 and 2, "The Rape of the Lock"

    A.   Blank verse

    B.   Heroic couplet

    C.   Free verse

    D.   Octava rima

Answer: B. Heroic couplet
This excerpt is an example of a heroic couplet, two successive lines of iambic pentameter poetry with end rhyme. Blank verse is unrhymed poetry written in iambic pentameter. Free verse is poetry that does not have any predictable meter or rhyming pattern. Octava rima is a specific eight-line stanza of poetry whose rhyme scheme is abababcc.

11. Which of these is not an example of personification?
(Rigorous)

- A. "The wind stood up and gave a shout. He whistled on his two fingers." —"The Wind" by James Stephens

- B. "Only the champion daisy trees were serene. After all, they were part of a rain forest already two thousand years old and scheduled for eternity, so they ignored the men and continued to rock the diamondbacks that slept in their arms. It took the river to persuade them that indeed the world was altered." —*Tar Baby* by Toni Morrison

- C. "I am silver and exact. I have no preconceptions/Whatever I see, I swallow immediately/Just as it is, unmisted by love or dislike./ I am not cruel, only truthful" —"Mirror" by Sylvia Plath

- D. "I heard a fly buzz when I died;/ The stillness round my form/Was like the stillness in the air/Between the heaves of storm." —"Dying" by Emily Dickinson

Answer: D. "I heard a fly buzz when I died;/ The stillness round my form/Was like the stillness in the air/Between the heaves of storm." —"Dying" by Emily Dickinson

Although the fly buzzes and the storm heaves, these are not examples of personification but rather descriptions of sounds. In the poem by James Stephens, the wind is standing, shouting, and whistling. In Morrison's excerpt, the trees are ignoring and rocking and the river is persuading. In Plath's excerpt, the mirror does not preconceive (think) but it does see and swallow and has human-like characteristics ("not cruel, only truthful").

12. In the O. Henry short story "The Gift of the Magi," the young husband sells his watch to buy hair combs for his wife and the young wife sells her hair to buy a watch fob for her husband. This is an example of
    (Easy)

    A. Irony

    B. Parallelism

    C. Epiphany

    D. Stream of consciousness

Answer: A. Irony
Irony is the disparity between what happens and what is expected to happen. In this example, the irony of situation is the contrast between the expected results and the actual results. Parallelism is the arrangement of ideas in phrases, sentences, and paragraphs that balance one element with another of equal importance and similar wording. Epiphany is a sudden realization or what Wordsworth would call "moments" of revelation or "spots of time." Stream of consciousness is a style of writing that reflects the mental processes of the characters, expressing at times jumbled memories, feelings, and dreams. In "The Jilting of Granny Weatherall" by Katherine Anne Porter, the protagonist is dying but reliving events in her life through a stream-of-consciousness monologue.

13. Which of the following is not true about plot?
    (Average)

    A. One way to analyze plot is to note the action verbs

    B. Plot is the sequence of events in the story

    C. Character is a literary element that often propels the plot

    D. Plot is found only in fiction

Answer: D. Plot is found only in fiction
The literary elements of a story are found in both fiction, where the story is imaginary, and non-fiction, where the story is real. For example, a biography or autobiography will relate a sequence of events with characters and settings.

14. **What literary element is most noticeable in this excerpt from James Baldwin's *Sonny's Blues*?**
    (Easy)

    When he was about as old as the boys in my class his face had been bright and open, there was a lot of copper in it; and he'd had wonderfully direct brown eyes, and great gentleness and privacy. I wonder what he looked like now. He had been picked up, the evening before, in a raid on an apartment downtown, for peddling and using heroin.

    A. Character

    B. Setting

    C. Plot

    D. Mood

Answer: A. Character
Using in 3rd person point of view, James Baldwin introduces the main character of *Sonny's Blues* through the eyes of his narrator by combining physical description (bright and open face, copper) with emotional description (great gentleness and privacy).

15. What literary element is most noticeable in this excerpt from the short story "A Clean Well Lighted Place" by Ernest Hemingway?
(Average)

Turning off the electric light he continued the conversation with himself, it was the light of course but it is necessary that the place be clean and pleasant. You do not want music. Certainly you do not want music. Nor can you stand before a bar with dignity although that is all that is provided for these hours. What did he fear? It was not a fear or dread, it was a nothing that he knew too well. It was all a nothing and a man was a nothing too. It was only that and light was all it needed and a certain cleanness and order. Some lived in it and never felt it but he knew it all was nada y pues nada y nada y pues nada. Our nada who art in nada, nada be thy name thy kingdom nada thy will be nada in nada as it is in nada. Give us this nada our daily nada and nada us our nada as we nada our nadas and nada us not into nada but deliver us from nada; pues nada. Hail nothing full of nothing, nothing is with thee. He smiled and stood before a bar with a shining steam pressure coffee machine.

- A. Theme
- B. Character
- C. Mood
- D. Dialogue

Answer: C. Mood
Mood is the feeling or atmosphere of a work. It can be created through setting, objects, details, images, characters, and words. In this short story, Hemingway uses his typical clipped style, simple diction, and repetition to create a feeling of gloom. Theme is the main idea the author is trying to convey, which the mood facilitates. Character would be the person in the story. Dialogue would be a conversation between two or more people, which is a major part of this story, but not this excerpt.

16. **Which of these would be an effective way to describe the theme of Shakespeare's *Romeo and Juliet*?**
    (Average)

    A. Star-crossed lovers

    B. Family prejudices can cause grief and death

    C. Romantic love can be an overpowering force

    D. Love

Answer: C. Romantic love can be an overpowering force
Theme is the underlying main idea of a piece of literature. It is the controlling idea that the plot, characters, setting, and mood develop. Themes should never be single words (love) or clichés (star-crossed lovers). They should reflect the purpose of the author and be supported by all the other elements (plot, character, setting, mood). While family prejudices do set the plot in action, the main idea is that romantic love can be an overpowering force.

17. **In which genre did Tennessee Williams write?**
    (Easy)

    A. Essays

    B. Drama

    C. Poetry

    D. Short Story

Answer: A. Essays
Tennessee Williams was a twentieth century playwright who won the Pulitzer Prize for *A Streetcar Named Desire* and for *Cat on a Hot Tin Roof*. Born in Mississippi, Thomas Lanier Williams eventually moved to New Orleans, and his plays have southern settings with memorable characters.

18. Which of the following is not a typical literary device used in drama?
    (Average)

    A. Aside

    B. Soliloquy

    C. Chorus

    D. Sermon

Answer: D. Sermon
Of the responses provided, a sermon is not a typical literary device used in drama, although sermons can certainly be dramatic and some plays can be sermon-like. An aside is when a character speaks directly and briefly to the audience, often to indicate what that character is thinking or about to do. In *Othello*, Iago often tells the audience how he intends to achieve his goals. A soliloquy is a long speech given by an actor on stage to reveal his inner thoughts. The most famous is Hamlet's "To be or not to be" soliloquy in Act 3 of Shakespeare's play. In Greek drama, the chorus would comment on the characters and events in the play. A modern use of the chorus can be seen in Woody Allen's movie *Mighty Aphrodite*.

19. What type of literary work is non-fiction prose focusing on a topic and propounding a definite point of view and authoritative tone?
    (Easy)

    A. Epistle

    B. Essay

    C. Epic

    D. Allegory

Answer: B. Essay
A genre credited to Michel de Montaigne in the sixteenth century, an essay is a short discussion of a topic in prose. The word is taken from French *essai*, which at the time of the Renaissance meant "trial" or an "attempt." An epistle is a letter that was not necessarily intended for public distribution but that, because of the fame of the sender and/or recipient, became public domain. An epic is a long poem recounting actions, travels, adventures and heroic episodes. An allegory is a figurative work whose surface narrative carries a secondary and often metaphorical meaning.

20. **Which of the following authors is not considered an essayist?**
    (Average)

    A. Charles Lamb

    B. Ralph Waldo Emerson

    C. Michel de Montaigne

    D. Robert Browning

Answer: D. Robert Browning
A genre credited to Michel de Montaigne in the sixteenth century, an essay is a short discussion of a topic in prose. The word is taken from French *essai*, which at the time of the Renaissance meant "trial" or an "attempt." Charles Lamb, an eighteenth century English essayist, had a strong influence on the genre. In the nineteenth century, American writer Ralph Waldo Emerson converted many of his speeches to essays, including his famous "Self-Reliance." Robert Browning was a nineteenth-century British poet and playwright.

21. **Which of the following can be called a fable?**
    (Average)

    A. *Animal Farm* by George Orwell

    B. *Canterbury Tales* by Geoffrey Chaucer

    C. *Pride and Prejudice* by Jane Austen

    D. *Gulliver's Travels* by Jonathan Swift

Answer: A. *Animal Farm* by George Orwell
Because its main characters are animals who illustrate human-like characteristics and foibles, George Orwell's *Animal Farm* is considered an allegorical fable. *Canterbury Tales* by Geoffrey Chaucer is a collection of stories, of which the "Nun's Priest's Tale" is a fable. Jane Austen's *Pride and Prejudice* has none of the characteristics of a fable. Swift's novel *Gulliver's Travels* has been called everything from a satire to a classic children's story to an allegory depending on the view of the reader or literary critic; however, it is not a fable.

22. Which playwright changed the idea of the tragic hero to include the common man?
(Average)

    A.   Arthur Miller

    B.   Sophocles

    C.   William Shakespeare

    D.   Jean Racine

Answer: A. Arthur Miller
In plays like *All My Sons* and *Death of a Salesman*, Arthur Miller adapted Aristotle's view on the classic hero to show how middle-class characters gain and lose their nobility through their own nature rather than class or high birth. Sophocles' heroes, such as Oedipus, fulfilled Aristotle's view of the classic tragic hero. Shakespeare's tragedies all focus on men of noble birth or high standing: *King Lear; Hamlet, Prince of Denmark; Julius Caesar; Othello*. Seventeenth-century French playwright Jean Racine wrote tragedies about noble characters; for example, *Britannicus* focuses on Agrippa, the mother of the Roman emperor Nero.

23. On *The Rocky and Bullwinkle Show* cartoon show, dashing hero Dudley Do-Right of the Mounties saves the wholesome heroine Nell Fenwick who has been tied to the railroad tracks by the mean villain Snidely Whiplash. What type of comedy is this?
    (Rigorous)

    A.   Farce

    B.   Burlesque

    C.   Comic drama

    D.   Melodrama

Answer: D. Melodrama
With stereotypical characters and elements (good guys wear white; bad guys wear black) and syrupy sentimentality, melodrama is a form of comedy that relies on unlikely events to emphasize the conflict between pure good and pure evil. Comic drama, with its serious and light elements, originated in the Middle Ages under the auspices of the Catholic Church, which tried to reach the common people via mystery and morality plays. The modern equivalent would be television's "dramedies," which present a serious plot with comic elements. Farce is noted for its low humor and physical comedy. Burlesque comedy is another example of low comedy; it began in nineteenth-century America as theatrical entertainment marked by parody but later devolved into striptease shows.

24. What is the purpose of an octave in a Petrarchan sonnet?
    (Rigorous)

    A.   It states a problem, asks a question, or expresses an emotion

    B.   It introduces the characters and sets the tone

    C.   It resolves a problem, answers a question, or responds to an emotion

    D.   It sets the mood and rhyme pattern for the rest of the poem

Answer: A. It states a problem, asks a question, or expresses an emotion
The Petrarchan sonnet generally has a two-part theme. The first eight lines, called the octave, state a problem, ask a question, or express an emotional tension. The last six lines, called the sestet, resolve the problem, answer the question, or relieve the tension. The rhyme scheme of the octave is abbaabba; that of the sestet varies.

25. **Which type of sonnet uses the quatrain-and-couplet pattern with an abab bcbc cdcd ee rhyming pattern?**
    (Rigorous)

    A.   The Spenserian sonnet

    B.   The Petrarchan sonnet

    C.   The English sonnet

    D.   The Italian sonnet

Answer: A. The Spenserian sonnet
A form of the English sonnet created by Edmond Spenser combines the English form and the Italian. The Spenserian sonnet follows the English quatrain-and-couplet pattern but resembles the Italian sonnet in its rhyme scheme, which is linked: abab bcbc cdcd ee. The Italian/Petrarchan sonnet has an octave with a abbaabba rhyme scheme and a sestet with a variable rhyme scheme. The English sonnet has three quatrains with independent rhyme schemes followed by a rhyming couplet.

26. Which type of sonnet is exemplified by the following?
(Rigorous)

What guyle is this, that those her golden tresses
She doth attyre under a net of gold,
And with sly skill so cunningly them dresses,
That which is gold or haire may scarse be told?
Is it that mens frayle eyes, which gaze too bold,
She may entangle in that golden snare;
And, being caught, may craftily enfold
Their weaker harts, which are not wel aware?
Take heed therefore, myne eyes, how ye doe stare
Henceforth too rashly on that guilefull net,
In which if ever ye entrapped are,
Out of her bands ye by no meanes shall get.
Fondnesse it were for any, being free,
To covet fetters, though they golden bee!

A. English sonnet

B. Italian sonnet

C. Spenserian sonnet

D. Petrarchan sonnet

Answer: C. Spenserian sonnet
"Sonnet 37" is an example of the sonnet form developed by Edmund Spenser. The Spenserian sonnet follows the English quatrain-and-couplet pattern but resembles the Italian sonnet in its rhyme scheme, which is linked: abab bcbc cdcd ee. The English sonnet has three quatrains with independent rhyme schemes followed by a rhyming couplet. The rhyme scheme of this Shakespearean sonnet is ababcdcdefefgg. The Italian/Petrarchan sonnet has an octave with a abbaabba rhyme scheme and a sestet with a variable rhyme scheme.

27. Which of the following is not a ballad?
(Rigorous)

A. "The Rime of the Ancient Mariner" by Samuel Taylor Coleridge

B. "The Walrus and the Carpenter" by Lewis Carroll

C. "Do Not Go Gentle Into That Good Night" by Dylan Thomas

D. "La Belle Dame Sans Merci" by John Keats

Answer: C. "Do Not Go Gentle Into That Good Night" by Dylan Thomas
"Do Not Go Gentle Into That Good Night" is a villanelle, a type of poetry invented in France in the sixteenth century and used mostly for pastoral songs. It has an uneven number of tercets (usually five) rhyming aba, with a final quatrain rhyming abaa. A ballad is a story told or sung, usually in verse and accompanied by music. Literary devices found in ballads include the refrain, or repeated section, and incremental repetition, or anaphora, for effect.

28. Which of the following is not an allusion?
(Average)

A. After being on restriction for a week, John started calling his bedroom Elba

B. Chocolate is my Achilles' heel

C. You're tilting at windmills if you expect me to cooperate

D. He served as peacemaker between the two foes

Answer: D. He served as peacemaker between the two foes
By calling his room "Elba," John is alluding to Napoleon's isle of exile. An "Achilles' heel" is a weak spot or vulnerability and alludes to Achilles, the Greek warrior who as a child was held by his ankles and dipped in the River Styx by his mother for protection. He was later killed in the Trojan War when he was shot in the heel by an arrow. "Tilting at windmills" alludes to Don Quixote, who in his quest, would attack windmills thinking they were giants. The phrase means an unwinnable fight or attacking imaginary foes. As used here, "peacemaker" is meant to be taken literally—one who makes peace—and does not allude to the Biblical phrase "Blessed are the peacemakers."

29. Which type of literary genre encompasses fictional stories involving children or animals that come in contact with supernatural beings via magic?
(Easy)

   A.   Fairy tales

   B.   Myths

   C.   Fables

   D.   Folktales

Answer: A. Fairy Tales
Fairy tales are lively fictional stories involving children or animals that come in contact with super beings via magic. Fairy tales provide happy solutions to human dilemmas. The fairy tales of many nations are peopled by trolls, elves, dwarfs, and pixies, child-sized beings capable of fantastic accomplishments. Myths are traditional tales of cultural significance that deal with gods, supernatural beings and attempt to explain natural phenomena. In fables, animals talk, feel, and behave like human beings. Fables always have a moral, and the animals depict specific people or groups indirectly. Folk tales include tall tales and legends that combine fact and fiction and use exaggeration.

30. Which of the following is not a tall tale?
(Average)

   A.   While traveling in a covered wagon, Pecos Bill fell out unnoticed by his family near the Pecos River and was raised by coyotes

   B.   In "The Swollen Tree," a rattlesnake bites a tree, which swells so large that a hunter is able to build a five-room house from the wood

   C.   In North Carolina, Bear Creek got its name from the season that Daniel Boone killed ninety-nine bears along its water

   D.   To scratch an itch, Babe the Blue Ox would rub against a cliff

Answer: C. In North Carolina, Bear Creek got its name from the season that Daniel Boone killed ninety-nine bears along its water
The story about Daniel Boone is legend, which is a tale based on a real person that is part fact and part fiction. The rest are tall tales, which are humorously exaggerated stories about impossible events.

31. Which genre of American Literature wrote about the common man and his socioeconomic problems in a non-sentimental way?
(Rigorous)

    A.   Native American Literature

    B.   Colonial Literature

    C.   Romantic Literature

    D.   Realistic Literature

Answer: D. Realistic Literature
The Realists wrote about the common man and his socioeconomic problems in a non-sentimental way. Characteristics of Native American literature include reverence for and awe of nature and the interconnectedness of the elements in the life cycle. Its themes include the hardiness of the native body and soul, remorse for the destruction of the native way of life, and the genocide of many tribes by the encroaching settlement and Manifest Destiny policies of the U.S. government. Colonial literature was neoclassical and emphasized order, balance, clarity, and reason; it had strong ties to British literature at the time. Romantic literature emphasized the individual. Emotions and feelings were validated, and nature acted as an inspiration for creativity. Romantics hearkened back to medieval, chivalric themes and ambiance.

32. **Whose writings from early American literature relate the hardships of crossing the Atlantic and the misery and suffering of the first colonists?**
    (Easy)

    A.   Anne Bradstreet

    B.   William Bradford

    C.   William Byrd

    D.   Thomas Paine

Answer: B. William Bradford
William Bradford's excerpts from *The Mayflower Compact* relate vividly the hardships of crossing the Atlantic in a tiny vessel, the misery and suffering of the first winter, the approaches of the American Indians, the decimation of the colonists' ranks, and the establishment of the Bay Colony of Massachusetts. Anne Bradstreet's poetry describes colonial New England life. From her journals, modern readers learn about the everyday life of the early settlers, the hardships of travel, and the responsibilities of different groups and individuals in the community. William Byrd's journal *A History of the Dividing Line,* concerning his trek into the Dismal Swamp separating the Carolinian territories from Virginia and Maryland makes quite lively reading. Thomas Paine's pamphlet *Common Sense* spoke to the American patriots' common sense in dealing with issues in the cause of freedom; this word is considered part of the Revolutionary Period.

33. **Which of the following is a characteristic of literature during the Revolutionary Period?**
    (Average)

    A.   Fiction, such as poems and novels

    B.   Fiction, such as short stories and plays

    C.   Non-fiction, such as essays, pamphlets, speeches, documents, and epistles

    D.   Non-fiction, such as dictionaries, encyclopedias, and atlases

Answer: C. Non-fiction, such as essays, pamphlets, speeches, documents, and epistles
While a wide variety of literature was written during the American Revolutionary Period, the most representative examples are the non-fiction essays, pamphlets, speeches, documents, and epistles.

34. Who was not considered one of the "Fireside Poets"?
(Average)

    A.   Nathaniel Hawthorne

    B.   James Russell Lowell

    C.   Henry Wadsworth Longfellow

    D.   John Greenleaf Whittier

Answer: A. Nathaniel Hawthorne
Nathaniel Hawthorne was a prolific writer of the Romantic period of American literature, but he was not a poet. The poetry of the "Fireside Poets"—James Russell Lowell, Oliver Wendell Holmes, Henry Wadsworth Longfellow, and John Greenleaf Whittier—was recited by American families and read during the long New England winters. In "The Courtin'," Lowell used Yankee dialect to tell a story. Spellbinding epics by Longfellow (such as *Hiawatha*, *The Courtship of Miles Standish*, and *Evangeline*) told of adversity, sorrow, and ultimate happiness in a uniquely American fashion. The poem "Snowbound" by Whittier relates the story of a captive family isolated by a blizzard and stresses family closeness.

35. **Which of the following is the story of an accident at sea that results in the death of one of the ship's officers, Claggert, a slug of a fellow who had taken a dislike to a young, affable, shy sailor. Captain Vere must hang the sailor for the death of Claggert but knows that his punishment is not just. However, an example must be given to the rest of the crew so that discipline can be maintained?**
(*Average*)

   A.   *Moby Dick*

   B.   *Billy Budd*

   C.   *The House of Seven Gables*

   D.   "On the Duty of Civil Disobedience"

Answer: B. *Billy Budd*
Herman Melville offers up the succinct tale of *Billy Budd* and his Christ-like sacrifice to the black-and-white maritime laws on the high seas. His more famous novel, *Moby Dick*, follows a crazed Captain Ahab on his Homeric odyssey to conquer the great white whale that has outwitted him and his whaling crews time and again. *The House of the Seven Gables* by Nathaniel Hawthorne deals with kept secrets, loneliness, societal pariahs, and the triumph of love over horrible wrongs. Henry David Thoreau wrote passionately about his objections to the interference of government in the life of the individual in "On the Duty of Civil Disobedience."

36. **Identify the style/period of this poem?**
    (Rigorous)

    **It was many and many a year ago,
    In a kingdom by the sea,
    That a maiden there lived whom you may know
    By the name of Annabel Lee;
    And this maiden she lived with no other thought
    Than to love and be loved by me.**

    A.   Neoclassicism

    B.   Romanticism

    C.   Realism

    D.   Naturalism

Answer: A. Neoclassicism
Written by Edgar Allan Poe in 1849, this poem falls within the Romantic period. It is typical of Poe's style in its poetic structure (ballad) and theme (the death of a beautiful woman and the concept of ideal love).

37. Who is the author of this poem?
(Easy)

Because I could not stop for Death,
He kindly stopped for me;
The carriage held but just ourselves
And Immortality.

We slowly drove, he knew no haste,
And I had put away
My labor, and my leisure too,
For his civility.

- A. Emily Dickinson
- B. John Greenleaf Whittier
- C. Walt Whitman
- D. James Lowell

Answer: A. Emily Dickinson

Emily Dickinson left her literary fingerprints on a vast array of poems, all but three of which were never published in her lifetime. Her themes of introspection and attention to nature's details and wonders are world-class works, as in the case here. "Because I Could Not Stop for Death" is a typical poem by Dickinson, both in style—short lines, first-person point of view—and theme. In this instance, she personifies Death in her examination of mortality.

38. Which of these was written during the Medieval Period of British Literature? *(Average)*

    A.   *Beowulf*

    B.   *Le Morte d'Arthur*

    C.   *Samson Agonistes*

    D.   *The Rape of the Lock*

Answer: B. *Le Morte d'Arthur*
Thomas Malory's *Le Morte d'Arthur,* written during the Medieval Period of British Literature (1066-1485), brought together extant tales from Europe concerning the legendary King Arthur, Merlin, Guinevere, and the Knights of the Round Table. *Beowulf* was anonymously written by Christian monks during the Anglo-Saxon Period, which spanned six centuries and ended with the Norman Conquest in 1066. John Milton wrote the social commentary Samson Agonistes in the seventeenth century. Alexander Pope wrote *The Rape of the Lock,* a mock epic, in the eighteenth century.

39. In what period of British literature was this verse written?
    (Rigorous)

    From fairest creatures we desire increase,
    That thereby beauty's rose might never die,
    But as the riper should by time decease,
    His tender heir might bear his memory:
    But thou, contracted to thine own bright eyes,
    Feed'st thy light's flame with self-substantial fuel,
    Making a famine where abundance lies,
    Thyself thy foe, to thy sweet self too cruel.
    Thou that art now the world's fresh ornament
    And only herald to the gaudy spring,
    Within thine own bud buriest thy content
    And, tender churl, makest waste in niggarding.
    Pity the world, or else this glutton be,
    To eat the world's due, by the grave and thee.

    A. Anglo-Saxon Period

    B. Medieval Period

    C. Renaissance Period

    D. Seventeenth century

Answer: C. Renaissance Period
Written by William Shakespeare during the Renaissance Period, this sonnet illustrates the pattern he developed. Shakespeare dispensed with the octave/sestet format of the Italian sonnet and invented his three quatrains, one heroic couplet format that follows the abab, cdcd, efef, gg rhyme scheme.

40. Identify the period of British Literature for this excerpt.
(Average)

No man is an island,
Entire of itself.
Each is a piece of the continent,
A part of the main.
If a clod be washed away by the sea,
Europe is the less.
As well as if a promontory were.
As well as if a manner of thine own
Or of thine friend's were.
Each man's death diminishes me,
For I am involved in mankind.
Therefore, send not to know
For whom the bell tolls,
It tolls for thee.

- A. Renaissance
- B. Seventeenth century
- C. Eighteenth century
- D. Nineteenth century

Answer: B. Seventeenth century
Taken from John Donne's *Meditations*, written in 1624, this excerpt was not originally written as a poem. The famous lines "no man is an island" and "for whom the bell tolls" tie together the two themes of isolation and mortality.

41. **Which of the following were not authors during the Enlightenment of the eighteenth century?**
    (Average)

    A. Alexander Pope

    B. Daniel Defoe

    C. James Boswell

    D. William Blake

Answer: D. William Blake
With his mystical pre-Romantic poetry, William Blake ushered in the Romantic Age and its revolution against Neoclassicism. During the Enlightenment, neoclassicism became the preferred writing style, especially for Alexander Pope. New genres, evidenced in works such as *The Diary of Samuel Pepys*, the novels of Daniel Defoe, the periodical essays and editorials of Joseph Addison and Richard Steele, and Alexander Pope's mock epic *The Rape of the Lock*, demonstrate the diversity of expression during this time.

42. **Which of these authors did not write during the British Romantic Period of the nineteenth century?**
    (Rigorous)

    A. George Eliot

    B. Jane Austen

    C. Alfred, Lord Tennyson

    D. Charlotte Bronte

Answer: C. Alfred, Lord Tennyson
Alfred, Lord Tennyson was a poet who typified the Victorian period. During the British Romantic period, Mary Anne Evans, also known as George Eliot, wrote several important novels: her masterpiece *Middlemarch*, *Silas Marner*, *Adam Bede*, and *Mill on the Floss*. Jane Austen wrote her novels, including *Pride and Prejudice* and *Sense and Sensibility*. Charlotte Bronte wrote *Jane Eyre*.

43. **Which of the following is not a characteristic of the Pre-Raphaelites?**
    (Rigorous)

    A.   Reacted against Victorian materialism

    B.   Affirmed the neoclassical conventions of academic art

    C.   Produced earnest, quasi-religious works

    D.   Encouraged artists and writers to practice each other's art

Answer: B. Affirmed the neoclassical conventions of academic art
The Pre-Raphaelites, a group of nineteenth-century English painters, poets, and critics, reacted against Victorian materialism and denounced the neoclassical conventions of academic art by producing earnest, quasi-religious works. Medieval and early Renaissance painters up to the time of the Italian painter Raphael inspired the group. They encouraged each other to expand their talents and skills by practicing different art forms. For example, Dante Gabriel Rossetti wrote poems and painted.

44. **Which of the following was not a dramatist of the twentieth century?**
    (Easy)

    A.   George Bernard Shaw

    B.   Arthur Miller

    C.   Tom Stoppard

    D.   Henrik Ibsen

Answer: D. Henrik Ibsen
Henrik Ibsen (1828–1906) was a Norwegian playwright of the nineteenth century, whose famous words include *A Doll's House* and *An Enemy of the People*. George Bernard Shaw (1856–1950) was an Irish playwright whose great works include *St. Joan* and *Major Barbara*. Arthur Miller (1915–2005) was an American playwright whose famous works include *Death of a Salesman* and *The Crucible*. Tom Stoppard (born 1937) is a British playwright whose famous words include *Rosencrantz and Guildenstern Are Dead* and *Travesties*.

45. **Which of the following French authors has not won the Nobel Prize for Literature?**
    (Rigorous)

    A. Albert Camus

    B. Eugene Ionesco

    C. Jean-Paul Sartre

    D. Samuel Beckett

Answer: B. Eugene Ionesco
Eugene Ionesco (1909–1994) did not win a Nobel Prize for Literature. He was a French playwright of the Theatre of the Absurd movement; his works include *The Bald Soprano* and *Rhinoceros*. Albert Camus (1913–1960), the author of *The Stranger* and *The Plague*, received the Nobel Prize in Literature in 1957. Jean-Paul Sartre (1905–1980), a philosopher and author whose existential philosophy grew from the works of Heidegger and was influenced by WWII, received the Nobel Prize for Literature in 1964. His famous works include *Being and Nothingness* and *No Exit*. Samuel Beckett (1906–1989) wrote plays and novels and is most famous for the absurdist play *Waiting for Godot*. He received the Nobel Prize for Literature in 1969.

46. **What changed occurred in adolescent literature in the seventeenth century?**
    (Average)

    A. Literature began to be written specifically for the young

    B. The Puritans in Europe were able to ban all literature aimed at children

    C. Publishers began to offer large stipends to authors of children's literature

    D. More authors began to write long novels for young readers

Answer: A. Literature began to be written specifically for the young
The late seventeenth century brought the first literature that specifically targeted the young. For example, Pierre Peril's *Fairy Tales*, Jean de la Fontaine's retellings of famous fables, Mme. d'Aulnoy's novels based on old folktales, and Mme. de Beaumont's *Beauty and the Beast* were written to delight as well as instruct young people. In England, publisher John Newbury was the first to publish a literary line for children, such as a translation of Perrault's *Tales of Mother Goose*; *A Little Pretty Pocket-Book*, "intended for instruction and amusement" but decidedly moralistic and bland in comparison to the previous century's chapbooks; and *The Renowned History of Little Goody Two Shoes*, allegedly written by Oliver Goldsmith for a juvenile audience.

47. Children's literature that functions at the concrete operations stage, focuses on the "good person," has plots dependent on external rewards, and exhibits all five needs from Maslow's hierarchy is appropriate for what reading level?
    (Rigorous)

    A.   Fifth and Sixth Grades

    B.   Seventh and Eighth Grades

    C.   Ninth Grade

    D.   Tenth to Twelfth Grade

Answer: A. Fifth and Sixth Grades
Most 11 to 12 year olds will appreciate works such as Roald Dahl's *Charlie and the Chocolate Factory* and Elizabeth Speare's *The Witch of Blackbird Pond* because they combine the characteristics of multiple learning theories, function at the concrete operations stage (Piaget), have the "good person" orientation (Kohlberg), still highly dependent on external rewards (Bandura), and exhibit all five needs from Maslow's hierarchy.

48. Which of the following is not a challenge in selecting books at the appropriate reading level?
    (Average)

    A.   The diverse interests of students

    B.   The diverse reading levels of students

    C.   The availability of realistic fiction

    D.   The lack of high-interest books for on- or below-level readers

Answer: D. The lack of high-interest books for on- or below-level readers
A large number of high-interest, low-readability books have flooded the market. The plethora of high-interest books reveals how desperately schools have failed to produce on-level readers and how the market has adapted to that need. Because of rapid social changes, topics that once did not interest young people until they reached their teens—suicide, gangs, and homosexuality—are now the subjects of books for younger readers.

49. Which of the following works deal with the subject of immigration?
(Average)

   A.   *Uncle Tom's Cabin*

   B.   *The Joy Luck Club*

   C.   *Go Tell It on the Mountain*

   D.   *Catch-22*

Answer: B. *The Joy Luck Club*
Immigration has been a popular topic in literature from the time of the Louisiana Purchase in 1804. A more recent addition to this genre is Amy Tan's *The Joy Luck Club* (1989), which deals with the problems faced by Chinese immigrants. *Uncle Tom's Cabin* (1852) by Harriet Beecher Stowe is often referred to as the book that started the Civil War because of its stance on antislavery. *Go Tell It on the Mountain* (1953) by James Baldwin is a semi-autobiographical coming-of-age story about the role of the church in the lives of African Americans. *Catch-22* (1961) by Joseph Heller is a satirical novel set during the end of World War II.

50. Which period of literature is patterned after the writings of Greeks and Romans, does not exalt the self, and focuses on the group rather than the individual?
(Easy)

   A.   Neoclassicism

   B.   Romanticism

   C.   Realism

   D.   Naturalism

Answer: A. Neoclassicism
Patterned after the great writings of classical Greece and Rome, neoclassic literature is characterized by a balanced, graceful, well-crafted, refined, and elevated style. In neoclassical writing, the self is not exalted. Focus is on the group rather than the individual. Romantic literature emphasizes the individual. Emotions and feelings are validated, and nature acts as an inspiration for creativity. Realistic writing deals with the common man and his socioeconomic problems in a non-sentimental way. Naturalism is realism pushed to its limit—writing that exposes the underbelly of society, usually the lower-class struggles.

51. **Which of the following is not a member of the first generation of Romantic writers?**
    (Rigorous)

    A.   William Wordsworth

    B.   Samuel Taylor Coleridge

    C.   Ralph Waldo Emerson

    D.   Percy Bysshe Shelley

Answer: D. Percy Bysshe Shelley
Percy Bysshe Shelley is a member of the second generation of Romantic writers; this group stressed personal introspection and a love of beauty and nature as requisites for inspiration. The first generation of Romantic writers (Wordsworth, Coleridge, Emerson, Thoreau, Poe) maintained that the scenes and events of everyday life and the speech of ordinary people were the raw material from which poetry could and should be made.

52. **Which term can be defined as words or sentences that help readers determine the meanings of words?**
    (Easy)

    A.   Prior knowledge

    B.   Context clues

    C.   Comprehension

    D.   Cues

Answer: B. Context clues
Context clues are words or sentences that help readers determine the meanings of words. Context clues can appear within the sentence itself, within the preceding and/or following sentence(s), or within the passage as a whole. Prior knowledge is using all of one's prior experiences, learning, and development when entering a specific learning situation or attempting to comprehend a specific text. Sometimes prior knowledge can be erroneous or incomplete. Prior knowledge includes the accumulated positive and negative experiences that readers have acquired, both in and out of school. Comprehension occurs when the reader correctly interprets the text and constructs meaning from it. Cues are used to direct and monitor reading comprehension.

53. In an essay on "The Cask of the Amontillado," Jorge writes this sentence: "This short story by Poe is not his best example of horror fiction. I prefer 'The Tell-Tale Heart' because of the way the author builds suspense and adds tension throughout the story." Which type of reading response does this illustrate?
(Rigorous)

    A.   Emotional

    B.   Interpretive

    C.   Critical

    D.   Evaluative

Answer: C. Critical
This is an example of a critical response, which makes a value judgment about the quality of a piece of writing. In an emotional response, readers can identify with the characters and situations so as to project themselves into the story. Interpretive responses lead to inferences about character development, setting, or plot; analysis of style elements; outcomes derivable from information provided in the narrative; and assessment of the author's intent. An evaluative response considers such factors as how well the piece of literature represents its genre, how well it reflects the social/ethical mores of society, and how well the author has approached the subject with regard to freshness and slant.

54. In her AP English class, Miriam has written an essay comparing and contrasting the works of John Steinbeck as they reflect the social and economic times of the first half of the twentieth century. What type of literary response does this represent?
    (Rigorous)

    A. Emotional

    B. Interpretive

    C. Critical

    D. Evaluative

Answer: D. Evaluative
This is an example of an evaluative response, which considers such factors as how well the piece of literature represents its genre, how well it reflects the social/ethical mores of society, and how well the author has approached the subject with regard to freshness and slant. Evaluative responses are harder to detect and are rarely made by any but a few advanced high school students. In an emotional response, readers can identify with the characters and situations so as to project themselves into the story. Critical responses involve making value judgments about the quality of a piece of literature. Interpretive responses lead to inferences about character development, setting, or plot; analysis of style elements; outcomes derivable from information provided in the narrative; and assessment of the author's intent.

55. What is the SQ3R method of reading comprehension?
    (Average)

    A. Study, Quiz, Recite, Review, Remember

    B. Survey, Question, Read, Recite, Recognize

    C. Survey, Question, Read, Recite, Review

    D. Summarize, Question, Read, Recall, Review

Answer: C. Survey, Question, Read, Recite, Review
Organized study models teach students to locate main ideas and supporting details, to recognize sequential order, to distinguish fact from opinion, and to determine cause/effect relationships. One such model is the SQ3R method, a technique that enables students to learn the content of even large amounts of text (Survey, Question, Read, Recite, and Review Studying).

56. **Ms. Prince is reading and scoring portfolios that students submitted after their study of Romeo and Juliet. What is the correct term for this process?**
 (Rigorous)

    A. Evaluation

    B. Planning

    C. Assessment

    D. Interpretation

Answer: A. Evaluation
The correct term is evaluation, which is the process of judging the students' responses to determine how well they are achieving particular goals or demonstrating reading skills. Assessment is the practice of collecting information about students' progress. Planning is formulating a plan of action. Interpretation is to explain the meaning of something.

57. **After Mr. Whitson's class has left, he writes brief comments about each student's participation in discussion for that day. What type of assessment is this?**
 (Average)

    A. Formal

    B. Informal

    C. Holistic

    D. Formative

Answer: B. Informal
This is informal assessment, which is the use of observation and other non-standardized procedures to compile anecdotal and observational data/evidence of children's progress. Informal assessment includes but is not limited to checklists, observations, and performance tasks. Formal assessment is composed of standardized tests and procedures carried out under prescribed conditions. Formal assessments include state tests, standardized achievement tests, NAEP tests, and the like. Holistic scoring is a method by which trained readers evaluate a piece of writing for its overall quality. Formative assessment is a self-reflective process that promotes student attainment of goals.

Direction: Read this poem and answer questions 58–62:

Out, Out—

The buzz-saw snarled and rattled in the yard
And made dust and dropped stove-length sticks of wood,
Sweet-scented stuff when the breeze drew across it.
And from there those that lifted eyes could count
Five mountain ranges one behind the other
Under the sunset far into Vermont.
And the saw snarled and rattled, snarled and rattled,
As it ran light, or had to bear a load.
And nothing happened: day was all but done.
Call it a day, I wish they might have said
To please the boy by giving him the half hour
That a boy counts so much when saved from work.
His sister stood beside them in her apron
To tell them "Supper." At the word, the saw,
As if to prove saws knew what supper meant,
Leaped out at the boy's hand, or seemed to leap—
He must have given the hand. However it was,
Neither refused the meeting. But the hand!
The boy's first outcry was a rueful laugh.
As he swung toward them holding up the hand
Half in appeal, but half as if to keep
The life from spilling. Then the boy saw all—
Since he was old enough to know, big boy
Doing a man's work, though a child at heart—
He saw all spoiled. "Don't let him cut my hand off—
The doctor, when he comes. Don't let him, sister!"
So. But the hand was gone already.
The doctor put him in the dark of ether.
He lay and puffed his lips out with his breath.
And then—the watcher at his pulse took fright.
No one believed. They listened at his heart.
Little—less—nothing!—and that ended it.
No more to build on there. And they, since they
Were not the one dead, turned to their affairs.

—Robert Frost

58. Identify the figure of speech in the first line of the poem "The buzz-saw snarled and rattled in the yard"?
(Easy)

   A.   Assonance

   B.   Onomatopoeia

   C.   Apostrophe

   D.   Metaphor

Answer: B. Onomatopoeia
This line is an example of onomatopoeia. Words like "buzz," "snarled," and "rattled," imitate the sound of the buzz saw. Assonance is the repetition of vowel sounds. Apostrophe addresses an abstraction. A metaphor is an implied comparison.

59. Identify the figure of speech in this line: "So. But the hand was gone already."
(Rigorous)

   A.   Metonymy

   B.   Allusion

   C.   Personification

   D.   Synecdoche

Answer: D. Synedoche
A synecdoche is a figure of speech in which the word for part of something is used to mean the whole. In this line "hand" is meant to represent the boy's life. Not only was the hand gone but also the boy's life. Metonymy is using the name of something to represent something closely associated with it, such as using "The Pentagon" to mean the military. Allusion is a reference to someone or something in literature or history. Personification is giving human-like characteristics to something not human.

60. What type of poetry is "Out, Out—"?
(Average)

    A.   Narrative

    B.   Dramatic

    C.   Epic

    D.   Lyric

Answer: A. Narrative
"Out, Out—" is a narrative poem because its main purpose is to tell a story. It has characters, setting, plot, and a narrative arc from exposition to denouement. Dramatic poetry presents the voice of a character speaking directly to the audience. It reveals key aspects of the character's psyche and sheds insight on the situation at hand. The audience takes the part of the silent listener, passing judgment and giving sympathy at the same time. In epic poetry, the action takes place in a social sphere rather than a personal sphere. Lyric poetry tends to be short poems expressing the thoughts and feelings of a single speaker. It also has musical qualities, which was the original meaning of lyric poetry.

61. What literary element is represented by the poem's title "Out, Out—"?
(Rigorous)

    A.   Oxymoron

    B.   Personification

    C.   Onomatopoeia

    D.   Literary allusion

Answer: D. Literary allusion
The title of this poem "Out, Out—" alludes to lines in Shakespeare's Macbeth when the king hears news of his wife's death: "Out, out, brief candle!" By using this literary allusion, Frost is foreshadowing the death of the young boy. Personification is giving human characteristics to inanimate objects. Onomatopoeia is the naming of a thing or action by a vocal imitation of the sound associated with it, such as "buzz" or "hiss." An oxymoron is a contradiction in terms deliberately employed for effect. An oxymoron is usually seen in a qualifying adjective whose meaning is contrary to that of the noun it modifies, such as "wise folly."

62. **Which of the following would be an interpretive question to ask students about this poem?**
    (Rigorous)

    A. How does Frost make the buzz-saw look sinister?

    B. How do you feel about apparent indifference of the people in the last two lines?

    C. Compare this poem to "Sir Patrick Spence," a traditional Scottish ballad. How do these poems represent narrative poetry?

    D. Does Frost's poem effectively convey the theme of the effect of a meaningless death?

Answer: A. How does Frost make the buzz-saw look sinister?
By asking about the style of the poet, choice A is asking an interpretive question. Response B is asking an emotional question, asking students to identify with the characters. Choice C is an evaluative question, asking students to compare how well these poems represent a particular style. Choice D is a critical question, asking students to make a value judgment.

Directions: Read this poem and answer questions 63–67.

The Lake Isle of Innisfree

I will arise and go now, and go to Innisfree,
And a small cabin build there, of clay and wattles made:
Nine bean-rows will I have there, a hive for the honey-bee;
And live alone in the bee-loud glade.

And I shall have some peace there, for peace comes dropping slow,
Dropping from the veils of the morning to where the cricket sings;
There midnight's all a glimmer, and noon a purple glow,
And evening full of the linnet's wings.

I will arise and go now, for always night and day
I hear lake water lapping with low sounds by the shore;
While I stand on the roadway, or on the pavements grey,
I hear it in the deep heart's core.

—William Butler Yeats

63. What literary element is used in the line "I hear lake water lapping with low sounds by the shore"?
(Easy)

    A.   Alliteration

    B.   Caesura

    C.   Assonance

    D.   Sprung rhythm

Answer: A. Alliteration
Alliteration occurs when the initial sounds of a word (beginning with either a consonant or a vowel) are repeated in close succession. In this line, the "l" sound is repeated. Assonance occurs when the vowel sound within a word matches the same sound in a nearby word, but the surrounding consonant sounds are different. Caesura is a pause, usually signaled by punctuation, in a line of poetry. Sprung rhythm, invented and used extensively by the poet Gerard Manley Hopkins, consists of variable meter, which combines stressed and unstressed syllables

64. **What type of poetry is "The Lake Isle of Innisfree"?**
(Rigorous)

- A. Dramatic
- B. Narrative
- C. Epic
- D. Lyric

Answer: D. Lyric
"The Lake Isle of Innisfree" is a lyric poem because it is a short poem expressing the thoughts and feelings of a single speaker. It also has musical qualities, which was the original meaning of lyric poetry. A narrative poem tells a story. It has characters, setting, plot, and a narrative arc from exposition to denouement. Dramatic poetry presents the voice of a character speaking directly to the audience. It reveals key aspects of the character's psyche and sheds insight on the situation at hand. The audience takes the part of the silent listener, passing judgment and giving sympathy at the same time. In epic poetry, the action takes place in a social sphere rather than a personal sphere.

65. **What literary element is represented by the poem's lines: "Nine bean-rows will I have there, a hive for the honey-bee/And live alone in the bee-loud glade.**
(Rigorous)

- A. Literary allusion
- B. Personification
- C. Onomatopoeia
- D. Oxymoron

Answer: A. Literary allusion
The "nine bean-rows" is a literary allusion to Thoreau's bean patch, as is the rest of the line reminiscent of Thoreau's *Walden* and the idea of escaping into nature. Personification is giving human characteristics to inanimate objects. Onomatopoeia is the naming of a thing or action by a vocal imitation of the sound associated with it, such as "buzz" or "hiss." An oxymoron is a contradiction in terms deliberately employed for effect. An oxymoron is usually seen in a qualifying adjective whose meaning is contrary to that of the noun it modifies, such as "wise folly."

66. Which of the following would be an evaluative question to ask students about this poem?
(Rigorous)

- A. Does reading "The Lake Isle of Innisfree" remind you of any places you have been?

- B. Does Yeats achieve his purpose in conveying the picture of the lake isle?

- C. How is Yeats' poem an example of lyric poetry of the Victorian period?

- D. How does the diction of Yeats contribute to the musical quality of the poem?

Answer: C. How is Yeats' poem an example of lyric poetry of the Victorian period?

Choice C is an evaluative question because it asks readers to consider how well the piece of literature represents its genre. Choice A is an emotional question because it asks readers for personal identification. Choice B is a critical question because it asks readers to make a value judgment. Choice D is an interpretive question because it asks readers to examine style elements.

67. How can students determine the meaning of the word "wattles"?
(Average)

    A.   Using context clues of the preceding phrase "And a small cabin build there, of clay and wattle made" students can understand that it is a building material

    B.   Using prior knowledge, students will draw on their past experiences in nature and realize that it is something like clay

    C.   Using connotation, students will understand this it is a positive word

    D.   Using the poet's explanation in the next line with the phrase "nine bean-rows, students will understand that it is a type of plant

Answer: A. Using context clues of the preceding phrase "And a small cabin build there, of clay and wattle made" students can understand that it is a building material

One of the ways to determine meanings of unknown words is to examine the context of a word. In this line of poetry, Yeats is talking about building a cabin with two items: "of clay and wattles." The students can assume that it shares the same purpose as clay—to build a cabin. To confirm their definition, students can consult a dictionary and learn that wattles are "poles interwoven with sticks used in building." Not many students will be able to draw upon their prior knowledge to understand this word, and knowing that it has a positive connotation will not necessarily help them define it. Further, nine bean-rows has no connection to wattles and is part of another idea in the poem.

68. Which of the following is not an internal factor affecting Juan's language development?
(Rigorous)

    A.   Juan celebrates his 8th birthday

    B.   Juan had ear infections as a baby

    C.   Juan is the youngest of four children

    D.   Juan experienced developmental delays after a premature birth

Answer: C. Juan is the youngest of four children
Birth order is an external factor that affects language development. Age, medical problems, and physical development are internal factors.

69. **Which approach of language development is based on the idea that language ability is innate and develops through natural human maturation?**
    (Easy)

    A. Learning approach

    B. Linguistic approach

    C. Cognitive approach

    D. Sociocognitive approach

Answer: B. Linguistic approach
Formulated by Noam Chomsky in the 1950s, the linguistic approach believes that language ability is innate and develops through natural human maturation. The learning approach believes that language develops from learning the rules of language structures and applying them through imitation and reinforcement. This approach also assumed that language, cognitive and social developments were independent of each other. The cognitive approach believes that language knowledge derives from syntactic and semantic structures. The sociocognitive approach believes that language development results from the interaction of language, cognitive, and social knowledge as part of the whole human development.

70. **Which of the following would be an effective way to incorporate the sociocognitive approach to learning development in a classroom?**
    (Average)

    A. Provide opportunities for students to make oral presentations

    B. Encourage students to engage in silent reading

    C. Provide individualized online research activities

    D. Encourage students to keep journals

Answer: A. Provide opportunities for students to make oral presentations
As a result of the sociocognitive approach in the 1970s, a larger emphasis has been placed on verbal communication. Thus, oral presentations, conversations, discussions, and group work encourage social interaction and enable speakers to apply their cognitive skills. Silent reading and solitary activities, while valuable, are not the strongest ways to develop sociocognitive skills.

71. Ian drives a lorry through the streets of London, takes a lift to his second-floor flat, and eats bangers and mash for dinner. Maia drives a truck in Boston, uses the elevator to get to her fifth-floor apartment, and cooks hot dogs for dinner. What language influences are demonstrated by this scenario?
    (Average)

    A.   Social

    B.   Personal

    C.   Geographical

    D.   Genetic

Answer: C. Geographical
Geographical influences affect pronunciation and word choice. Social influences are imposed by family, peer groups, and mass media. Personal influences relate to individual growth and development. While genetics may affect language development, it is not the type of influence demonstrated in this scenario.

72. Which of the following is written in Middle English?
(Rigorous)

- A. HWÆT, WE GAR-DEna in geardagum,Þeodcyni nga þrym gefrunon,hu ða æþelingas ellen fremedon!

- B. But for to tellen yow of his array,His hors were goode, but he was nat gay.Of fustian he wered a gyponAl bismotered with his habergeon,For he was late ycome from his viage,And wente for to doon his pilgrymage.

- C. To be, or not to be: that is the question:Whether 'tis nobler in the mind to sufferThe slings and arrows of outrageous fortune,Or to take arms against a sea of troubles,And by opposing end them?

- D. I have been assured by a very knowing American of my acquaintance in London, that a young healthy child well nursed is at a year old a most delicious, nourishing, and wholesome food, whether stewed, roasted, baked, or boiled.

Answer: B. But for to tellen yow of his array,His hors were goode, but he was nat gay.Of fustian he wered a gyponAl bismotered with his habergeon,For he was late ycome from his viage,And wente for to doon his pilgrymage.

Choice B is from the "Knight's Tale" by Geoffrey Chaucer, written at the end of the fourteenth century, which is the Middle English period. Choice A is an excerpt from *Beowulf*, written around 1000 AD in the West Saxon dialect of Old English. Choice C is an excerpt from the famous soliloquy in *Hamlet* by William Shakespeare, written in the early 1600s, during the Modern English period. Choice D is an excerpt from "A Modest Proposal," a satirical essay written by Jonathan Swift in 1729.

73. Which of the following is not true about the growth of the English language?
(Rigorous)

- A. Spanish and English colonization contributed to the growth of English in Western hemisphere
- B. Modern inventions such as radios, television, and movies have helped to standardize pronunciation
- C. Technology has expanded English vocabulary
- D. English is easier to learn because of its rules and structure

Answer: D. English is easier to learn because of its rules and structure
Although the rules of English give it structure, the exceptions to the rules complicate learning the language. While the language has lost many of its unnecessary inflections, it has borrowed words from other cultures and with these words come rules from the lender language. Spanish and English are the major languages of the Western hemisphere because of colonization. Radios, television, and movies have reduced many aspects of regional dialects. Because of technology, the English language is constantly growing; words like "google," "e-mail," and "blog" are some of the more ubiquitous neologisms.

74. In what way is the English language slower to change?
(Rigorous)

- A. Spelling
- B. Vocabulary
- C. Pronunciation
- D. Syntax

Answer: D. Syntax
English syntax relies on word order. For example, the standard sentence structure is subject, verb, object: Martina baked the cake. If the order of the words changed, so would the meaning: The cake baked Martina. The English language does not rely on inflections as much as other languages so syntax is more important and thus less likely to change. Spelling changes occur quickly, as text messaging and Twitter demonstrate. Hundreds of new words enter the vocabulary yearly, making English a dynamic language. Because of communication and technology, pronunciation has become more standardized although local, regional, and national dialects still differentiate cultures.

75. **What three parts can form a word?**
    (Average)

    A. A prefix, a neologism, and a syllable

    B. A root word, a suffix, and a syllable

    C. A syllable, a neologism, and a suffix

    D. A prefix, a root word, and a suffix

Answer: D. A prefix, a root word, and a suffix
A prefix is a syllable added to the beginning of a word to add meaning. For example, the prefix "un" means "not" as in "unnatural." A root word is the base linguistic unit that can stand alone, as in "nature." A suffix is a syllable added to the end of a word to add meaning. In this example, the suffix "al" is an inflectional suffix that changes the base word to an adjective.

76. **In the word "absenteeism," what does the suffix "ism" mean?**
    (Rigorous)

    A. Resembling

    B. The act of

    C. Capable of

    D. The study of

Answer: B. The act of
Understanding the meanings of suffixes can help students define unfamiliar words. In "absenteeism," the suffix "-ism" means "the act of" and will help students understand "terrorism" and "pacificism." The suffix "-oid" means "resembling," as in words like "asteroid" or "spheroid." The suffixes "-able" and "-ible" mean capable of as in "portable" and "legible." The suffix "-logy" means "the study of" as is "cardiology" and "etymology."

77. **What is the definition of vernacular?**
    (Average)

    A. The history of a word

    B. A new word or phrase added to the vocabulary

    C. The language of a particular group or region

    D. An informal word or phrase used by a particular group

Answer: C. The language of a particular group or region
The language of a particular group of region in everyday conversation is called the vernacular. Similar to vernacular, a colloquialism is an informal word or phrase used by a particular group. Using contractions, for example, would be colloquial. The history of a word is called its etymology. Knowing the origins of a word can be very helpful in vocabulary study. A neologism is a new word or phrase added to the vocabulary. Recent neologisms include "twitter," "blogosphere," and "webinar." Technology and popular culture are two of the many driving forces that refresh our language.

78. **Which of the following is not true about spelling?**
    (Rigorous)

    A. English spelling is complicated because it does not follow the one-sound, one letter formula

    B. English spelling became easier with more phonetic representation of sounds

    C. The English adopted the Latin-based alphabet with changes from the Greeks and Romans

    D. English spelling became more standardized after the invention of the printing press

Answer B. English spelling became easier with more phonetic representation of sounds
Despite many attempts to nudge spelling into a more phonetic representation of sounds, all have failed for the most part. A good example is Noah Webster's *Spelling Book* (1783), which was a precursor to the first edition (1828) of his *American Dictionary of the English Language*.

79. Which of the following is a compound sentence?
(Average)

    A.   Neither Laurie nor Billy trusted the accountant with their tax return.

    B.   Although Shakespeare wrote in Modern English, high school students will have a difficult time with the language.

    C.   Spellcheckers can be your first line of defense against spelling errors and typos, but they are not infallible.

    D.   Vivi and Kasi offered to help but left before the meeting was over.

Answer: C. Spellcheckers can be your first line of defense against spelling errors and typos, but they are not infallible.
Choice C has two independent clauses (Spellcheckers can, They are) joined by a coordinating conjunction (but). Choice A is a simple sentence with one independent clause with a compound subject (Neither Laurie nor Billy). Choice B is a complex sentence with a dependent clause (Although Shakespeare wrote) and one independent clause (students will have). Choice D is a simple sentence with one independent clause that has a compound subject (Vivi and Kasi) and a compound verb (offered, left).

80. Which sentence uses subordination to show condition?
(Rigorous)

    A.   Because a database lists thousands of records, you must develop an effective search strategy.

    B.   Whether you consider yourself a good or bad speller, you must take time to proofread.

    C.   Although your friends might understand jargon, you should use concrete terms to write business letters.

    D.   Unless you object, we will proceed.

Answer: D. Unless you object, we will proceed.
The subordinating conjunction "unless" indicates a condition. In choice A, the subordinating conjunction "because" indicates cause. In choice B, the subordinating conjunction "whether" indicates choice. In choice C, the subordinating conjunction "although" indicates contrast.

81. Which of the following sentences has a dangling modifier?
(Rigorous)

    A.   Having worked sixty hours last week, John refused to work on Saturday.

    B.   To stay in touch with parents, telephone contacts are necessary.

    C.   If anyone has a cell phone, turn it off now.

    D.   After calling the faculty together, the principal announced her retirement this year.

Answer: B. To stay in touch with parents, telephone contacts are necessary.
Dangling modifiers occur when particular phrases do not relate to the subject being modified. In choice B, the phrase "To stay in touch with parents" does not modify the subject "contacts." In the other sentences, the opening participle phrases correctly modify the subjects.

82. Which of the following sentences has an error in parallel structure?
(Rigorous)

    A.   Colleen ate the ice cream with enthusiasm and in a hurry.

    B.   After hiking for hours, Joe sat down to rest and drink water.

    C.   Ms. Hill is expected to teach five sections, to counsel students, and to prepare lesson plans.

    D.   The book was exciting, well written, and it interested me.

Answer: D. The book was exciting, well written, and it interested me.
When a sentence contains a series of two or more related things or ideas, they should be expressed with a similar grammatical structure. In choice D, the three items joined by "and" are not parallel in form. "Exciting" and "well written" are adjectives, but "it interested me" is a clause. Make them all adjectives: "The book was exciting, well written, and interesting" or possibly add a second clause: "The book was exciting and well written, and it interested me."

83. **Choose the sentence in active voice.**
    (Average)

    A.   Your vacation request is approved, pending my signature.

    B.   Rain and slick road conditions caused the accident.

    C.   The assignment must be submitted by the end of the week.

    D.   Mrs. Johnson's automobile was inspected by the insurance company.

Answer: B. Rain and slick road conditions caused the accident.
A verb is in active voice when the subject is the doer of the action. In choice B, the rain and slick road conditions are the doers. In passive voice, the subject is the receiver of the action. A passive voice construction usually includes a form of the verb "to be" with a past participle. In choice A, the "request" is not doing anything. It is receiving the action and has the passive voice construction "is approved." In choice C, the assignment is not the doer and the passive voice construction is "must be submitted." In choice D, the automobile is not the doer, and the passive voice construction is "was inspected."

84. **Identify the sentence that is capitalized correctly.**
    (Easy)

    A.   Both my Father and Uncle John went fishing at the Washington dike last Thursday.

    B.   Because Labor Day is a federal holiday, all banks will be closed.

    C.   During the Spring Semester, the students from Washington academy made plans for the fall 2010 student orientation program.

    D.   The Late President Lyndon Johnson, who served in Office during the civil rights era, is remembered for his policies on integration.

Answer: B. Because Labor Day is a federal holiday, all banks will be closed.
Choice A should be "Both my father and Uncle John went fishing at the Washington Dike last Thursday." Choice C should be "During the spring semester, the students from Washington Academy made plans for the Fall 2010 Student Orientation Program." Choice D should be "The late President Lyndon Johnson, who served in office during the Civil Rights Era, is remembered for his policies on integration."

85. **What prewriting strategy is used to write down whatever comes to mind?** *(Easy)*

   A. Free writing

   B. Revising

   C. Editing

   D. Publishing

Answer: A. Free writing
Free writing is part of the first step of the writing process. Have students write down whatever comes to their minds without stopping to make connections or interrupt the flow of ideas. During the revision stage, students examine their work and make changes in sentences, wording, details, and ideas. During the editing stage, students proofread the draft for punctuation and mechanical errors. At the publishing stage, students may have their work displayed on a bulletin board, read aloud in class, or printed in a literary magazine or school anthology.

86. **What term is used in making a list of all ideas connected with your topic?** *(Easy)*

   A. Brainstorming

   B. Inspiration

   C. Breakthrough

   D. Innovation

Answer: A. Brainstorming
Brainstorming is a form of free writing in which writers make a list of all ideas connected to their topic. It works best when writers let their minds work freely as one idea leads to another. This can be done individually or within a group and is helpful for generating, focusing, and organizing ideas. During this process, writers may become inspired, make a breakthrough, or develop an innovative solution—but all of these come about through brainstorming.

87. Which of these is part of the editing stage?
(Average)

    A.   Proofread the draft for punctuation and mechanical errors

    B.   Use computer programs to check grammar and spelling

    C.   Share papers with peers

    D.   All of the above

Answer: D. All of the above
In the editing stage, student writers can use a number of techniques to review their compositions. While the reviewing stage focuses on ideas and organization, the editing stage examines the mechanics. What the writer or spellchecker may miss on a re-read, another writer may catch.

88. Which of these errors would be caught by a spellchecker?
(Average)

    A.   The decision was left up to he and I.

    B.   Tuan used the vaccuum cleaner to clean out the car.

    C.   Spellcheckers is useful for proofreading.

    D.   The Norman Conquest was in 1966.

Answer: B. Tuan used the vaccuum cleaner to clean out the car.
Computer spellcheckers will often stop as proper nouns such as Tuan, which writers can ignore or add to their spellchecker dictionaries. They will also catch misspelled words such as "vaccuum" ("vacuum"). However, spellcheckers will not catch incorrect pronoun case such as "to he and I" ("to him and me"). They will not check subject-verb errors, such as "Spellcheckers is..." ("Spellcheckers are..."). They will not catch wrong dates such as 1966 (1066).

89. **Which of the following is not a technique for creating a supportive classroom environment?**
    (Average)

    A. Provide several prompts or give students the freedom to write on a topic of their choice

    B. Respond to oral queries with a question whenever possible. Your response should be non-critical. Use positive, supportive language

    C. Create peer response/support groups that work on dissimilar writing assignments

    D. Provide the group with a series of questions to guide them through the group writing sessions

Answer: C. Create peer response/support groups that work on dissimilar writing assignments

Teachers can foster a supportive environment for writing by creating peer response and support groups that work on similar writing assignments. By having students look at what others have written about the same idea, they will be able to note the strengths and weaknesses of their own writing. If they were looking at dissimilar assignments, they would not be able to compare and contrast as effectively.

90. **When assessing and responding to student writing, which guideline is not formative?**
    (Rigorous)

    A. Reread the writing and note at the end whether the student met the objective of the writing task

    B. Responses should be non-critical and should use supportive and encouraging language

    C. Explain the criteria that will be used for assessment in advance

    D. For the first reading, use a holistic method, examining the work as a whole

Answer: D. For the first reading, use a holistic method, examining the work as a whole
Formative assessment is ongoing assessment used to determine how well students are working toward an objective or expectation. It includes the use of checklists, conferences, self-assessment, and focused observation. Summative assessment is the collection of data to measure the product of learning. It includes observations, performance work, unit project work, portfolio assessments, self-assessments, and additional selected assessment instruments and rubrics. Response D "For the first reading, use a holistic method, examining the work as a whole" is summative.

91. **What steps should you follow in gathering your data or information?**
    (Average)

    A. Keep a record of any sources consulted during the research process

    B. As you take notes, avoid unintentional plagiarism

    C. Summarize and paraphrase in your own words without the source in front of you

    D. All of the above

Answer: D. All of the above
Research can be an overwhelming process but it can be made easier if students are taught good habits in gathering data. By keeping a record of sources, they will be able to document their information correctly. As they take notes, they should put the information in their own words by either summarizing or paraphrasing. When making note of direct quotes, they should be sure to put quotation marks around information taken verbatim.

92. **Which of the following resources is the beginning point for many research projects?**
    (Average)

    A. Encyclopedias

    B. Dictionaries

    C. Databases

    D. The Internet

Answer: A. Encyclopedias
When conducting research, students can get an overview of their topic through a credible encyclopedia—hard copy or online. While Wikipedia is ubiquitous, students should be taught to examine the credibility of online information carefully. Dictionaries are useful for spelling, writing, and reading but have limited value as a research source. After encyclopedias, databases are the next step for students to search for in-depth credible information. To save time and effort, students should use Boolean operators to streamline their research process. The wide, wide world of the Internet poses challenges for fledgling researches. As with Wikipedia, students need to keep a critical eye on open source information.

93. **When searching online databases for information about the amount of money spent on bilingual education in private schools, which Boolean operators will generate the smallest number of hits?**
    (Rigorous)

    A. "bilingual education" not "private schools"

    B. "bilingual education" and "private schools"

    C. "bilingual education" or "private schools"

    D. "bilingual educat*" or "private schools"

Answer: B. "bilingual education" and "private schools"
By using "and," the search is narrowed and will retrieve records containing all of the words the operator separates. By using "not," the search is narrowed and will retrieve records for only the first term (bilingual education) and not for the second term (private schools). By using "or," the search is broadened and will retrieve records containing any of the words the operator separates: bilingual, education, private, schools. By using the asterisk, or wild card, the search is broadened and will retrieve records not only with bilingual, private, schools but any variation of "educat," such as educator, education, educating.

94. Which of the following materials are not considered a primary source? *(Average)*

- A. Literature and nonverbal materials, novels, stories, poetry, and essays from the period, as well as coins, archaeological artifacts, and art produced during the period

- B. Documents that reflect the immediate, everyday concerns of people: memoranda, bills, deeds, charters, newspaper reports, pamphlets, graffiti, popular writings, journals or diaries, records of decision-making bodies, letters, receipts, snapshots, and so on

- C. Books written on the basis of primary materials about the period of time

- D. Narrative accounts of events, ideas, and trends written with intentionality by someone contemporary with the events described

Answer: C. Books written on the basis of primary materials about the period of time

Primary sources are works, records, and the like that were created during the period being studied, such as archeological artifacts or diaries. Primary sources are the basic materials that provide the raw data and information. Secondary sources are works written after the period being studied and explain the primary sources. For example, the novel *Jane Eyre* would be a primary source but a collection of literary critiques about *Jane Eyre* would be a secondary source.

95. Dr. Alvin in thinking about buying a new car wants to research the following criteria: comfort, safety, and affordability. Which of the following would not qualify as primary research?
    (Rigorous)

    A. He visits a local dealership and test drives the latest model

    B. He picks up product brochures and creates a spreadsheet comparing and contrasting different models

    C. He visits Edmunds.com to check customer reviews

    D. He reads an article in Car and Driver that rates vehicles based on independent tests

Answer: D. He reads an article in Car and Driver that rates vehicles based on independent tests
The article in *Car and Driver* is based on research conducted by others and is a secondary source of information. By taking the test drive, compiling the spreadsheet, and reading the reviews, he is gathering data himself, which is primary research.

96. **Which of the following criteria would not be useful in determining the credibility of information found on a website?**
    (Average)

    A. Accuracy

    B. Timeliness

    C. Source

    D. Ease of use

Answer: D. Ease of use
Ease of use is a subjective measure affected by many factors, but it does not establish the credibility of the information found on a website. For researchers to rely on credible information, they must determine the accuracy of the information by evaluating the purpose of the site and understanding how the information was gathered. Another factor is timeliness. With the exception of historical data, information must be current and updated. The authority of the information—the source—can be determined in a number of ways, from looking at the web host to identifying the methods of research.

97. **What is another name for in-text documentation?**
    (Average)

    A. Parenthetical documentation

    B. Footnotes

    C. Works Consulted

    D. Bibliography

Answer: A. Parenthetical documentation
In the MLA style of documentation, used by humanities and education professionals, in-text documentation is often set off my parentheses. Other style sheets may use footnotes, but that system has become less common. A "Works Consulted" page and a Bibliography are lists of complete citation information placed at the end of a report.

98. **Which of the following is a correct bibliographic citation based on MLA style?**
    (Average)

    A. Wynne, Sharon. *English Language, Literature, and Composition: Teacher Certification Exam.* Boston: XAMonline, Inc., 2010.

    B. Sharon Wynne. *English Language, Literature, and Composition: Teacher Certification Exam.* Boston: XAMonline, Inc., 2010.

    C. Wynne, Sharon. (2010) *English language, literature, and composition: teacher certification exam.* Boston: XAMonline, Inc.

    D. Sharon Wynne, "English Language, Literature, and Composition: Teacher Certification Exam." Boston: XAMonline, Inc., 2010.

Answer: A. Wynne, Sharon. *English Language, Literature, and Composition: Teacher Certification Exam.* Boston: XAMonline, Inc., 2010.
In MLA style, a bibliographic citation includes this information in this order in this format for a single author. Use the hanging indent: the first line is flush left at the margin and the second and subsequent lines are indented. Note the punctuation as well.

Last Name, First Name. *Title and Subtitle of Book in Italics with Major Words Capitalized.* Place of Publication: Publisher, Date.

99. Which of the following would require a formal level of language?
(Average)

- A. A letter to the editor of the newspaper expressing appreciation for the police protection of a neighborhood event

- B. A report to the school board detailing the school's plan to improve the dropout rate of minority students

- C. A letter to the parents of students announcing the opening of the new school library

- D. A cover letter to the principal of a school requesting a job interview

Answer: B. A report to the school board detailing the school's plan to improve the dropout rate of minority students

A report to the school board detailing the school's plan to improve the dropout rate of minority students would require a formal level of language. Because of the purpose, content, and audience, this report would use a higher level of language, with longer sentences and a more sophisticated, technical, and precise language. Because of the subject matter of the letter to the editor and the letter to the parents, a more informal/conversational language level is appropriate. A cover letter requesting a job interview is a routine business message that does not require a formal level of language.

100. Which of the following are students assessing about their audience when they ask these questions: what is important to this group of people, what is their background, and how will that background affect their perception of your writing?
(Rigorous)

   A.   Constraints

   B.   Needs

   C.   Values

   D.   Demographics

Answer: C. Values
Before writing, students will want to assess their audience so they can tailor their writing to achieve their purpose. In assessing the values, writers are determining the beliefs of the readers. By assessing needs, writers are identifying what the audience requires. By assessing constraints, writers are identifying limitations. By assessing demographics, writers are identifying the quantifiable characteristics, such as age, gender, and education.

101. What are the three basic principles to follow to be convincing in writing or speaking?
(Average)

   A.   Emphasis, transition, and unity.

   B.   Coherence, emphasis, and transition.

   C.   Unity, coherence, and transition.

   D.   Unity, coherence, and emphasis

Answer: D. Unity, coherence, and emphasis
In writing or speaking, you can be convincing if you follow the three basic principles of unity, coherence, and emphasis. To achieve unity, all ideas must relate to the controlling thesis. To achieve coherence, use transitional words, phrases, sentences, and paragraphs to show relationship of ideas. To achieve emphasis, arrange ideas in strategic order to show their significance.

102. Which of the following would be an effective topic sentence to unify this paragraph?
    (Rigorous)

Club Palm Resort's beaches are beautiful, and the surrounding countryside is quite scenic. The quality of the food leaves a lot to be desired. Many vacationers enjoy the variety of outdoor activities and the instruction available in such sports as sailing and scuba diving. Unfortunately, security is poor; several vacationers' rooms have been broken into and their valuables stolen. Christmas in the Bahamas can make the thought of New Year's in Chicago bearable.

- A. Vacationers should take advantage of warmer climes for midwinter holidays.

- B. A vacation at Club Palm Resort has its good points and bad points.

- C. Club Palm Resort's isolation created dissatisfaction among some vacationers.

- D. For vacationers sick and tired of the frozen north, a week at Club Palm Resort can provide just the midwinter thaw they need.

Answer: D. For vacationers sick and tired of the frozen north, a week at Club Palm Resort can provide just the midwinter thaw they need.
Choice D provides a strong topic sentence that effectively unites the different ideas about a vacation at Club Palm Resort. Choice A does not relate to the resort. Choice B is too general to be effective. Choice C focuses on only one idea of the paragraph.

103. **What is the structural problem with this paragraph?**
    (Average)

    Club Palm Resort's isolation created dissatisfaction among some vacationers. The quality of the food was poor. People want a choice of entertainment in the evening. Most of us spent too much time together day after day. People expect to be able to go out for a meal if they feel like it.

    A.   Development

    B.   Coherence

    C.   Unity

    D.   Transition

Answer: B. Coherence
This paragraph lacks coherence. The topic sentence unifies the different ideas that follow, but the sentences don't have any meaningful connection to each other. This problem can be corrected by transitional words and phrases to show the relationship from one idea to another.

104. **Which of the following sentences uses transition to show contrasting ideas?**
    (Average)

    A.   In order to make the deadline, I will need to work throughout the weekend.

    B.   The camping trip was postponed because of bad weather; obviously, the scouts were very disappointed.

    C.   Americans are proud of their traditions, yet they are not afraid of new ideas.

    D.   Before Dana could attend the street fair, she needed to complete her literature essay on the poetry of Emily Dickinson.

Answer: C. Americans are proud of their traditions, yet they are not afraid of new ideas.
The conjunction "yet" is a transitional word that shows contrast. In choice A, the phrase "in order to" shows cause and effect. In choice B, the conjunctive adverb "obviously" provides clarification. In choice D, the subordinating conjunction "before" indicates time or sequence.

105. Which of the following is a disadvantage of a graphic message?
(Average)

    A.   Gives a quick overview of some quantifiable situation

    B.   Conveys a much shorter range of information

    C.   Relies on the ability of the viewer to understand the information

    D.   Provides visual appeal

Answer: C. Relies on the ability of the viewer to understand the information
With print messages, the viewer must be able to apply active reading skills, which may be difficult for less analytical readers. A graphic message does provide a quick overview of some quantifiable situation, and it does convey a much shorter range of information. A graphic message does provide visual appeal and has become a more prevalent way of communicating information.

106. Which type of written discourse implies the writer's ability to select vocabulary and arrange facts and opinions in such a way as to direct the actions of the listener/reader?
(Average)

    A.   Persuasive writing

    B.   Descriptive writing

    C.   Narrative writing

    D.   Basic expository writing

Answer: A. Persuasive writing
Persuasive writing implies the writer's ability to select vocabulary and arrange facts and opinions in such a way as to direct the actions of the listener/reader. Persuasive writing may incorporate exposition and narration as they illustrate the main idea. Basic expository writing simply gives information not previously known about a topic or is used to explain or define a topic. Facts, examples, statistics, and non-emotional information are presented in a formal manner. The tone is direct and the delivery objective rather than subjective. Descriptive writing centers on person, place, or object, using sensory words to create a mood or impression and arranging details in a chronological or spatial sequence. Narrative writing is developed using an incident or anecdote or a related series of events. Chronology, the 5 W's, topic sentence, and conclusion are essential ingredients.

107. **Which communication technique usually helps the speaker overcome speech anxiety by connecting with the attentive audience and easing feelings of isolation?**
    (Easy)

    A.   Eye contact

    B.   Gestures

    C.   Movement

    D.   Voice

Answer: A. Eye contact
Although many people may be intimidated by using eye contact when speaking to large groups, eye contact usually *helps* the speaker overcome speech anxiety by connecting with the attentive audience and easing feelings of isolation.

108. **What refers to the emotional appeal made by the speaker to the listener and emphasizes the fact that an audience responds to ideas with emotion?**
    (Easy)

    A.   Pathos

    B.   Logos

    C.   Ethos

    D.   Culture

Answer: A. Pathos
Pathos refers to the emotional appeal made by the speaker to the listener. It emphasizes the fact that an audience responds to ideas with emotion. Logos refers to the logic of the speaker's argument. It uses the idea that facts, statistics, and other forms of evidence can convince an audience to accept a speaker's argument. Ethos refers to the credibility of the speaker. It establishes the speaker as a reliable and trustworthy authority by focusing on the speaker's credentials. Culture is a shared system of beliefs, attitudes, values, and dispositions.

109. In 1959, Volkswagen ran an advertising campaign with the motto "Think Small." What type of advertising technique does this represent?
(Rigorous)

    A.   Compliment the consumer

    B.   Escape

    C.   Rebel

    D.   Statistical claim

Answer: C. Rebel
Because the typical aspiration is to think big, Volkswagen's motto "Think Small" uses the rebel technique because it associates products with behavior and lifestyles that oppose society's norms. McDonald's "You deserve a break today" would be an example of a compliment to the consumer. Advertisers flatter the consumer who is willing to purchase their product. By purchasing the product, the consumer is recognized by the advertiser for making a good decision with his or her selection. Calgon's advertisement to "Take Me Away" would encourage consumers to escape. Ivory soap's boast that it is "99 and 44/100% Pure" is a statistical claim.

110. Which of the following is an example of inductive reasoning?
(Rigorous)

- A. Maria speaks Spanish and English; Jacques speaks French and English; Vlad speaks Russian and English; therefore all students in my class are bilingual

- B. During the evening of September 3, Professor Plum was murdered in the library with the candlestick; Mrs. White saw Colonel Mustard leave the library that night with blood on his shoes; therefore Colonel Mustard was the murderer

- C. Tom's American-made Ford Escort is green; Dick's American-made Chevy Volt is green; Harry's American-made Dodge viper is green; therefore, all American-made cars are green

- D. All of the students in my class are bilingual; Blake is a student in my class; therefore Blake is bilingual

Answer: D. All of the students in my class are bilingual; Blake is a student in my class; therefore Blake is bilingual
Inductive reasoning is one of the two basic forms of valid reasoning. While deductive reasoning argues from the general to a specific instance, inductive reasoning argues from the particular to the general. In choice D, the argument moves from the general idea to a specific detail. Caution: be aware of faulty conclusions to these syllogisms.

111. Which of the following is an example of a post hoc fallacy?
(Rigorous)

   A.   When Simone sneezed, the tardy bell rang; therefore Simone caused the bell to ring

   B.   Liz's computer crashed after she installed the new software; therefore, the software caused the computer crash

   C.   When leaving the parking lot, Steve ran over some broken glass; on the way home, he got a flat tire; Steve reasons that the broken class caused his flat tire

   D.   Cameron doesn't like to use Facebook; he joins the computer club and notes that everyone uses Facebook; the club president ridicules others for not using the social networking site; Cameron decides to set up a Facebook page

Answer: D. Cameron doesn't like to use Facebook; he joins the computer club and notes that everyone uses Facebook; the club president ridicules others for not using the social networking site; Cameron decides to set up a Facebook page
Choice D is an example of a bandwagon fallacy. When faced with rejection, Cameron jumps on the Facebook bandwagon to conform to the views and positions of others. Choices A, B, and C are not examples of post hoc fallacies, whose conclusions are based on false or misleading cause-and-effect situations.

112. Which of the following is not written in first person point of view?
(Rigorous)

   A.   *The Catcher in the Rye*

   B.   *To Kill a Mockingbird*

   C.   *The Great Gatsby*

   D.   *The Old Man and the Sea*

Answer: D. *The Old Man and the Sea*
Ernest Hemingway used third person point of view in *The Old Man and the Sea* telling the story of a proud fisherman who wages a solitary battle against nature and mortality. J. D. Salinger uses first person point of view to have his narrator Holden Caulfield relate his personal story in *The Catcher in the Rye*. Harper Lee's young narrator in *To Kill a Mockingbird* is a five-year-old girl. F. Scott Fitzgerald's *The Great Gatsby* is seen through the eyes of its first-person narrator Nick Carraway.

113. Based on this brief excerpt from the short story "Miss Brill" by Katherine Mansfield, identify the point of view.
    (Average)

    Although it was so brilliantly fine—the blue sky powdered with gold and great spots of light like white wine splashed over the Jardins Publiques—Miss Brill was glad that she had decided on her fur. The air was motionless, but when you opened your mouth there was just a faint chill, like a chill from a glass of iced water before you sip, and now and again a leaf came drifting—from nowhere, from the sky. Miss Brill put up her hand and touched her fur. Dear little thing! It was nice to feel it again. She had taken it out of its box that afternoon, shaken out the moth-powder, given it a good brush, and rubbed the life back into the dim little eyes. "

    A. First person

    B. Second person

    C. Third person limited

    D. Third person omniscient

Answer: C. Third person limited
This excerpt is an example of third person limited since it talks about Miss Brill only. Before determining if the point of view was omniscient, you would need to read the entire story to see whether the author gets into the mind of all the characters (which, by the way, Mansfield does not)

114. **What are decisions or declarations based on observations or reasoning that express approval or disapproval?**
    (Average)

    A.   Judgments

    B.   Facts

    C.   Opinions

    D.   Conclusions

Answer: A. Judgments
Judgments are decisions or declarations based on observation or reasoning that express approval or disapproval. Facts are verifiable statements. Opinions are statements that must be supported in order to be accepted. Facts can be tested and verified, whereas opinions and judgments cannot. They can only be supported with facts. Conclusions are drawn as a result of reasoning. Whether arrived at through inductive or deductive reasoning, a conclusion is an analysis of the data.

115. **In a job interview, Colleen, a recent graduate, explains how proud she is that she worked twenty hours a week while attending college and still maintained a 3.2 GPA. She voices her disdain about other graduates who had no outside jobs and earned lower GPAs. Which form of bias is seen in this example?**
    (Rigorous)

    A.   Cultural bias

    B.   Racial bias

    C.   Professional bias

    D.   Unconscious bias

Answer: A. Cultural bias
Culture is a shared system of beliefs, attitudes, and values. In this example, Colleen has shown that she values her ability to achieve more than others who had fewer limitations.

Directions: Read the following essay and answer question 116:

The Insecure Sense of Femininity of Elisa
in John Steinbeck's Short Story "The Chrysanthemums"

(1) John Steinbeck's' short story "The Chrysanthemums," narrates an everyday series of events, but the emotional drama that Elisa goes through is very significant. (2) Elisa thinks of herself as strong, but she is, in fact, a very vulnerable woman. (3) She may be vital enough to have strong ambitions, but she is so insecure about her own femininity that she is finally unable to cope with the strain of transforming her life. (4) When we first see Elisa we get an immediate sense that she is hiding her sexuality from the rest of the world. (5) The speed and energy with which Elisa later seeks to transform herself really bring out the extent of her dissatisfaction with the role she has been playing. (6) But Elisa's new sense of herself does not last, for she has insufficient inner strength to develop into the mature, independent woman she would like to be.

116. Which sentence expresses the conclusion?
(Average)

- A. Sentence 1
- B. Sentence 3
- C. Sentence 5
- D. Sentence 6

Answer: A. Sentence 1
Sentence 1 is the conclusion because it provides the analysis of the supporting details presented in the paragraph. A conclusion does not have to be placed at the end of a paragraph. Sentences 3, 5, and 6 provide details to support the conclusion.

Directions: Read this paragraph and answer questions 117–120.

The argument that we need capital punishment in order to reduce the cost of maintaining the penal system is quite misplaced. There is no evidence that executing murderers will save us money. A number of studies of this question have shown that, on average, it costs about $50,000 per year to keep a maximum security offender in jail (Schneider, 2000; Ross and Sinclair 2006). A person who serves, say, a 25-year sentence, therefore, costs the state about $1,250,000. However, in countries which show some concern about the rights of the accused to a full and fair process, a system which has capital punishment for murder requires far more elaborate trials and a much lengthier and more expensive appeal process for capital offences than for non-capital offences. In addition, the cost of the execution itself is not insignificant. Recent studies by Gardner (2008) have shown that in the United States the cost of the various judicial processes and of the execution for convicted murderers is up to 30 percent higher than the cost of keeping them in jail for life. Other similar studies by McIntyre (2000) and Jackson (2005) have come to the same conclusion. There is, in other words, compelling reason seriously to question one of the most frequent claims made in support of capital punishment: that it will reduce costs significantly. In fact, if saving money is the main concern in the penal system, we should get rid of capital punishment immediately. *

*This text, which has been prepared by Ian Johnston of Malaspina University-College, Nanaimo, BC, is in the public domain and may be used, in whole or in part, without permission and without charge, released May 2000. [Ed. note: Sources are fictional and dates have been changed.]

117. What type of appeal is used in this paragraph?
   (Rigorous)

   A.   Logos

   B.   Ethos

   C.   Pathos

   D.   Both logos and ethos

Answer: A. Logos
By using objective data from credible resources, the author uses logos, a logical appeal, to craft the argument against capital punish. Even the author acknowledges that his argument presents "compelling reason seriously to question one of the most frequent claims made in support of capital punishment: that it will reduce costs significantly." If the author had used pathos, his argument would have appealed to the emotions. If the author had used ethos, he would have established his own credentials to establish his reliability.

118. In the essay on capital punishment, what is the purpose of the following sentence in the classical argument structure?
(Average)

There is no evidence that executing murderers will save us money.

A. Narration

B. Confirmation

C. Refutation

D. Summation

Answer: C. Refutation
In this sentence, the writer acknowledges and refutes opposing viewpoints. By anticipating objections, the writer strengthens his argument. In the narrative part of the classical argument, the writer would provide relevant background and explain the circumstances that produced the argument. In confirmation, the writer would logically develop the claims that support the thesis. In summation, writer concludes the argument with an effective summary.

119. In the essay on capital punishment, which of these sentences provides an effective summation?
(Rigorous)

- A. In addition, the cost of the execution itself is not insignificant.

- B. There is, in other words, compelling reason seriously to question one of the most frequent claims made in support of capital punishment: that it will reduce costs significantly.

- C. In fact, if saving money is the main concern in the penal system, we should get rid of capital punishment immediately.

- D. Recent studies by Gardner (1998) have shown that in the United States the cost of the various judicial processes and of the execution for convicted murderers is up to 30 percent higher than the cost of keeping them in jail for life.

Answer: B. There is, in other words, compelling reason seriously to question one of the most frequent claims made in support of capital punishment: that it will reduce costs significantly.
In the classical argument structure, the summation provides a strong conclusion. Response B echoes the thesis statement with the phrase "in other words" and repeats the main idea of his argument.

120. In the essay on capital punishment, what is the type of reasoning used?
(Average)

- A. Deductive

- B. Inductive

Answer: A. Deductive
The paragraph uses deductive logic by providing facts, research data, and quotations to reach a general conclusion.

Answer Key

1.	D	41.	D	81.	B
2.	C	42.	C	82.	D
3.	D	43.	B	83.	B
4.	D	44.	D	84.	B
5.	B	45.	B	85.	A
6.	D	46.	A	86.	A
7.	A	47.	A	87.	D
8.	C	48.	D	88.	B
9.	A	49.	B	89.	C
10.	B	50.	A	90.	D
11.	D	51.	D	91.	D
12.	A	52.	B	92.	A
13.	D	53.	C	93.	B
14.	A	54.	D	94.	C
15.	C	55.	C	95.	D
16.	C	56.	A	96.	D
17.	A	57.	B	97.	A
18.	D	58.	B	98.	A
19.	B	59.	D	99.	B
20.	D	60.	A	100.	C
21.	A	61.	D	101.	D
22.	A	62.	A	102.	D
23.	D	63.	A	103.	B
24.	A	64.	D	104.	C
25.	A	65.	A	105.	C
26.	C	66.	C	106.	A
27.	C	67.	A	107.	A
28.	D	68.	C	108.	A
29.	A	69.	B	109.	C
30.	C	70.	A	110.	D
31.	D	71.	C	111.	D
32.	B	72.	B	112.	D
33.	C	73.	D	113.	C
34.	A	74.	D	114.	A
35.	B	75.	D	115.	A
36.	A	76.	B	116.	A
37.	A	77.	C	117.	A
38.	B	78.	B	118.	C
39.	C	79.	C	119.	B
40.	B	80.	D	120.	A

Rigor Table

	Easy 16.7%	Average 40%	Rigorous 43.3%
Questions	3, 9, 12, 14, 17, 19, 29, 32, 37, 44, 50, 52, 58, 63, 69, 84, 85, 86, 107, 108	1, 6, 13, 15, 16, 18, 20, 21, 22, 30, 33, 34, 35, 38, 40, 41, 46, 48, 55, 57, 60, 67, 70, 71, 75, 77, 79, 83, 87, 88, 89, 91, 92, 94, 96, 97, 98, 99, 101, 103, 104, 105, 106, 113, 114, 116, 118, 120	2, 4, 5, 7, 8, 10, 11, 23, 24, 25, 26, 27, 28, 31, 36, 39, 42, 43, 45, 47, 49, 51, 53, 54, 56, 59, 61, 62, 64, 65, 66, 68, 72, 73, 74, 76, 78, 80, 81, 82, 90, 93, 95, 100, 102, 109, 110, 111, 112, 115, 117, 119

www.ingramcontent.com/pod-product-compliance
Lightning Source LLC
LaVergne TN
LVHW061312060426
835507LV00019B/2120